PATCHWORK ZOO

by Sara Nephew

Table of Contents

Special Thanks

In this book especially, I must give thanks to the many quilters who volunteered to test patterns and make quilts. Without their help and talents, this book would not be as varied, colorful, and exciting as I hope you find it.

They are:
Virginia Anderson, Annette Austin, Diane Coombs, Joan Dawson, Eda Lee Haas, Heki Hendrickson, Shirley Lyons, Tammy Mohiswarnath, Dee Morrow, Cleo Nollette, Carolann Palmer, Betty Parks, Judith Ann Pollard, Terri Shinn, Julie Stewart, Darlene Swenson, and Lynn Williams.

Credits

Unless expressly stated (see thanks at left), all the quilts in this book were designed, pieced and quilted by Sara Nephew.

Photography....Carl Murray

©Sara Nephew 1998
Clearview Triangle
8311 180th St. S. E.
Snohomish, WA 98296-4802 USA
Tel: 360-668-4151
Fax: 360-668-6338
E-mail: clearviewtriangle@compuserve.com

Library of Congress Catalog
Card Number: 97-94696
ISBN 0-9621172-7-7

INDEX OF 51 BLOCKS

PENGUIN

1½" finished square
5" x 9½" block with seam allowance

Cut for one block:

1.	1 background and 2 penguin	2" x 6½"	rectangle
2.	8 background and 4 penguin	2" x 2"	square
3.	1 background and 1 penguin	1¼" x 2"	rectangle

Directions: 1. Place a background 2" square on one end of a penguin 2" x 6½" rectangle and sew a diagonal seam as shown. Outside the stitching, trim fabric to a ¼" seam. Press to the rectangle. Place a background 2" square on the other end. Sew the opposite diagonal, trim and press. Make two of these.

2. Place a background and a penguin 2" square right sides together and sew a diagonal seam. Trim on one side of the stitching to a ¼" seam allowance. Press to the dark. This is a 2" half-square. (penguin beak and foot) Assemble according to the piecing diagram.

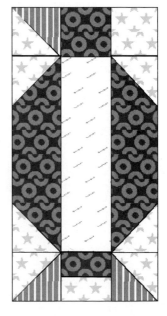

Piecing Diagram

FROG

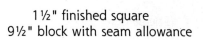

1½" finished square
9½" block with seam allowance

Cut for one block:

1.	1 frog	3½"	square
2.	1 background and 1 frog	2" x 12"	strip
3.	1 background	2" x 5"	rectangle
4.	1 background and 4 frog	2" x 3½"	rectangle
5.	2 background, 2 eye, 5 frog	2"	square

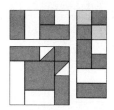

Piecing Diagram

Directions: 1. Sew the background and frog 2" x 12" strips together lengthwise. Press to the dark. From this set of strips, cut two 3½" sections and two 2" sections (hands and feet).

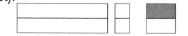

2. Place a background and frog 2" square right sides together and sew a diagonal seam. Trim on one side of the stitching to a ¼" seam allowance. Press to the dark. This is a 2" half-square. Assemble according to the piecing diagram.

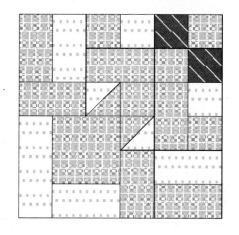

SCOTTY DOG

1½" finished square
9½" block with seam allowance

Cut for one block:

1.	1 dog	5" x 8"	rectangle
2.	1 background	5" x 3½"	rectangle
3.	1 background	5" x 2"	rectangle
4.	1 background and 4 dog	3½" x 2"	rectangle
5.	2 background and 3 dog	2"	square

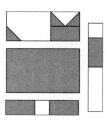

Piecing Diagram

Directions: 1. Place a dog 2" square at the right end of a background 3½" x 2" rectangle. Sew diagonally as shown. Trim outside the stitching to a ¼" seam. Press to the dark. Place a dog 2" square at the other end of the rectangle. Sew the opposite diagonal. Trim and press.

2. Place a dog 2" square over the lower left corner of the background 3½" x 5" rectangle and sew a diagonal seam as shown. Trim the seam to ¼" and press. Assemble according to the piecing diagram.

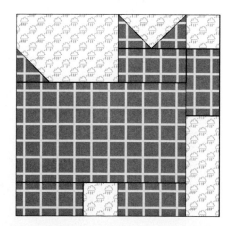

MOUSE

1½" finished square
5" x 15½" block with seam allowance

Cut for one block:

1.	1 mouse	5"	square
2.	1 background	3½" x 6½"	rectangle
3.	1 mouse	3½" x 5"	rectangle
4.	1 background and 1 mouse	1¼" x 6½"	strip
5.	7 background and 2 mouse	2"	square

Directions:

1. Place a background 2" square on two adjacent corners of the 5" mouse square and sew diagonal seams. Outside the stitching, trim to a ¼" seam. Press to the dark.

2. Sew background 2" squares on three corners of the 3½" x 5" mouse rectangle with diagonal seams as shown. Trim and press to the dark.

3. Sew the background and mouse 1¼" strips together lengthwise to make the mouse tail. Press to the dark. Place a 2" background square on the right end and sew diagonally as shown. Trim and press to the triangle. Assemble according to the piecing diagram.

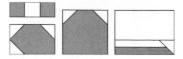

Piecing Diagram

PLAIN BIRD

1½" finished square
8" block with seam allowance

Cut for one block:

1.	1 background and 1 bird	5⅜"	square
2.	1 background	2" x 8"	rectangle
3.	1 background and 1 bird	2" x 5"	rectangle
4.	1 background	2" x 3½"	rectangle
5.	1 background and 1 bird	1¼" x 6"	strip
6.	1 background and 2 bird	2"	square

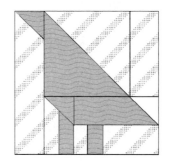

Directions:

1. Sew the background and bird 1¼" strips together lengthwise. Press to the dark. Then cut the following sections from this set of strips:

1.	2"	square
2.	3½"	rectangle

2. Cut the background and bird 5⅜" squares in half diagonally as shown. Sew one of each of the resulting triangles together to make a large half-square. (wing) *You will have one of each left over for another block.*

3. Place a bird 2" square on one end of a background 2" x 8" rectangle and sew a diagonal seam as shown. Trim and press. Place a background 2" square on one end of a bird 2" x 5" rectangle and sew a diagonal seam as shown. Trim and press.

4. Place a bird 2" square on one end of the 3½" strip section and sew a diagonal seam as shown. Assemble according to the piecing diagram.

Piecing Diagram

CHRISTMAS TREE

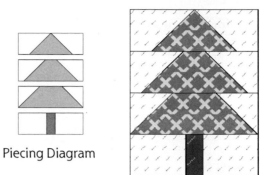

1½" finished square
5" x 6½" block with seam allowance

Cut for one block: *(Pin same-size pieces together and number)*

1.	1 trunk	1¼" x 2"	rectangle
2.	2 background	2" x 2¾"	rectangle
3.	4 background	2" x 2⅜"	rectangle
4.	2 background	2"	square
5.	1 tree	2" x 5"	rectangle
6.	1 tree	2" x 4¼"	rectangle
7.	1 tree	2" x 3½"	rectangle

Piecing Diagram

Directions:

1. Sew a 2" x 2⅜" (#3) background rectangle on either side of the trunk.

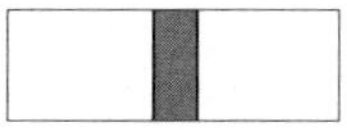

2. Place a background 2" square on the right end of the tree 2" x 5" (#5) rectangle. Sew diagonally as shown. Trim outside the stitching to a ¼" seam. Press to the dark. Place another background 2" square on the other end. Sew the opposite diagonal, trim and press.

3. Place a background 2" x 2⅜" (#3) perpendicular to the right end of a tree 2" x 4¼" (#6) rectangle as shown. Sew the diagonal seam, trim and press. Then do the same on the other side, sewing the opposite diagonal.

4. Place a background 2" x 2¾" (#2) rectangle perpendicular to the right end of a tree 2" x 3½" (#7) rectangle. Sew the diagonal seam, trim, and press. Sew all four rows together in order.

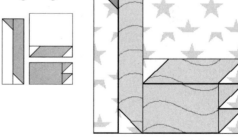

GOOSE

1½" finished square
9½" block with seam allowance

Cut for one block:

1.	1 background	5" x 6½"	rectangle
2.	1 goose	3½" x 5"	rectangle
3.	1 background and 1 goose	2" x 9½"	rectangle
4.	1 goose	2" x 6½"	rectangle
5.	5 background and 3 goose	2"	square

Piecing Diagram

Directions:

1. Place a goose 2" square on one end of a background 2" x 9½" rectangle and sew a diagonal seam as shown. Outside the stitching, trim fabric to a ¼" seam. Press to the rectangle. Make another one of these with reversed values.

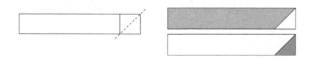

2. Place a background 2" square on one end of a goose 2" x 6½" rectangle and sew a diagonal seam as shown. Trim and press to the rectangle. Place a background 2" square on the other end. Sew the same diagonal, trim and press.

3. Place a background and goose square right sides together. Sew diagonally. Trim one side to a ¼" seam and press to the dark. Make two of these. This is a half-square. Assemble according to piecing diagram.

5

HIPPO

Cut for one block:

1.	1 hippo	6½"	square
2.	1 hippo	3½"	square
3.	1 background	2" x 5"	rectangle
4.	4 background and 1 hippo	2" x 3½"	rectangle
5.	3 background and 4 hippo	2"	square

Directions:

1. (A) Place a hippo 2" square on one end of a background 2" x 3½" rectangle and sew a diagonal seam as shown. Outside the stitching, trim to a ¼" seam. Press to the dark. (B) Make one of these with values reversed. (C) Place a hippo 2" square on one end of a background 2" x 3½" rectangle and sew the opposite diagonal seam as shown. Trim and press.

A.
B.
C.

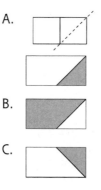

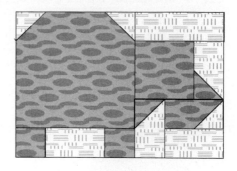

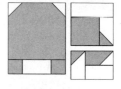

Piecing Diagram

2. Sew two background 2" squares on two corners of the 6½" hippo square with a diagonal seam as shown. Trim and press to the dark. Assemble according to the piecing diagram.

RHINOCEROS

Cut for one block:

1.	1 rhino	6½" x 8"	rectangle
2.	1 rhino	3½"	square
3.	3 background and 1 rhino	2" x 3½"	rectangle
4.	1 background and 1 rhino	1¼" x 8"	strip
5.	5 background and 4 rhino	2"	square

Directions:

1. Sew the background and rhino 1¼" strips together lengthwise. Press to the dark. Then cut the following sections from this set of strips:

1.	2	2" section
2.	1	3½" section

2. (A) Place a rhino 2" square on one end of the background 2" x 3½" rectangle and sew a diagonal seam as shown. Trim and press. (B) Make one with reverse values. Take this and place another 2" background square on the other end. Sew the opposite diagonal, trim and press.

A.
B.

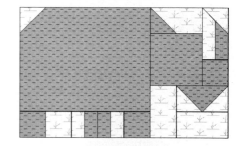

Piecing Diagram

3. Place a background 2" square on the right end of the 3½" strip section (rhino strip on the bottom) and sew a diagonal seam as shown. Outside the stitching, trim fabric to a ¼" seam. Press to the triangle.

4. Place a background 2" square on the upper left corner of the rhino 6½" x 8" rectangle. Sew a diagonal seam as shown. Assemble according to the piecing diagram.

HIPPO YAWNING

1½" finished square
8" x 11" block with seam allowance

Cut for one block:

1.	1 hippo	6½"	square
2.	1 hippo	3½"	square
3.	5 background and 1 hippo	2" x 3½"	rectangle
4.	3 background and 6 hippo	2"	square

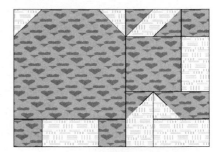

Directions:

1. (A) Place a hippo 2" square on one end of a background 2" x 3½" rectangle and sew a diagonal seam as shown. Outside the stitching, trim fabric to a ¼" seam. Press to the dark. (B) Make one of these with values reversed. (C) Place a hippo 2" square on one end of a background 2" x 3½" rectangle and sew a diagonal seam in the opposite direction. Put a hippo 2" square on the other end and sew the same diagonal again. Trim and press.

A.

B.

C.

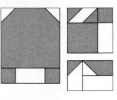

Piecing Diagram

2. Sew 2" background squares on two corners of the hippo 6½" square with diagonal seams as shown. Assemble according to the piecing diagram.

PANDA

1½" finished square
11" x 15½" block with seam allowance

Cut for one block:

1.	1 white	5" x 6½"	rectangle
2.	2 black	3½" x 6½"	rectangle
3.	2 background	2" x 6½"	rectangle
4.	4 white and 1 background	2" x 5"	rectangle
5.	2 background and 2 black	2" x 3½"	rectangle
6.	1 white and 1 black	1¼" x 2"	rectangle
7.	3 white, 7 background and 12 black	2"	square

Directions:

1.(A) Place a background 2" square on one end of a white 2" x 5" rectangle and sew a diagonal seam as shown. Outside the stitching, trim fabric to a ¼" seam. Press to the dark. Place another background square on the other end. Sew the opposite diagonal, trim and press. Make 2 of these (panda cheeks). (B) Make one with a white rectangle and black squares (chin). (C) Sew four black squares diagonally onto the corners of a white 5" x 6½" rectangle (belly).

A.

B.

C.

2. Sew one background square onto the upper right corner of a black 3½" x 6½" rectangle diagonally as shown. (shoulder) Make a right and a left. Assemble according to the piecing diagram.

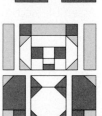

Piecing Diagram

Cut for one block:

1.	1 background and 1 boat	3⅞"	square
2.	1 boat	3½" x 5"	rectangle
3.	1 sky	2" x 11"	strip
4.	1 roof	2" x 8"	rectangle
5.	1 background and 1 boat	2" x 6½"	rectangle
6.	2 background	2" x 4¼"	rectangle
7.	1 background	1¼" x 11"	strip
8.	1 boat	1¼" x 2"	rectangle
9.	10 background and 7 water	2"	square

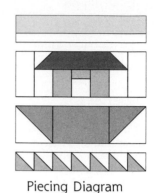

Piecing Diagram

Directions:

1. Sew the two 11" strips together lengthwise for the sky. Cut the 3⅞" background and boat squares diagonally and sew the resulting triangles together as shown. Then sew them to the 3½" x 5" boat rectangle.

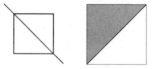

2. Sew the background and boat 2" x 6½" rectangles together lengthwise. Press to the dark. Then cut two 2¾" sections from this set of strips.

3. Place a background 2" square on one end of the 2" x 8" roof rectangle. Sew diagonally, trim outside the stitching to a ¼" seam, and press to the dark. Place another background square on the other end of the rectangle and sew the opposite diagonal.

4. Place a water and background 2" square right sides together and sew a diagonal seam. Trim on one side of the stitching to a ¼" seam allowance. Press to the dark. This is a 2" half-square. Make seven of these. Assemble according to the piecing diagram.

BUTTERFLY

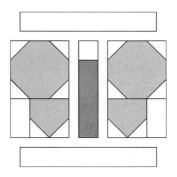

1½" each square
11" block with seam allowances

Cut for one block:

1.	2 butterfly	5"	square
2.	2 butterfly	3½"	square
3.	2 background*	2" x 11"	rectangle
4.	1 butterfly	2" x 6½"	rectangle
5.	2 background	2" x 3½"	rectangle
6.	13 background	2"	square

Leave off the bottom strip in the Noah's Ark Quilt.

Directions:

1. Place a background 2" square on one corner of a butterfly 5" square. Sew diagonally. Trim outside the stitching to leave a ¼" seam. Press to the dark. Do the same to the other three corners. Make two of these.

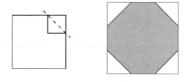

2. Place a background 2" square on one corner of a butterfly 3½" square. Sew diagonally. Trim the seam and press. Place a 2" square on a corner next to the first corner and sew diagonally again. Trim and press. Make two of these. Sew a background 2" x 3½" rectangle to the right and left to make a right and left bottom butterfly wing as shown.

3. Sew a background 2" square to the butterfly 2" x 6½" rectangle. Assemble the Butterfly block according to the piecing diagram. Add antennae as desired.

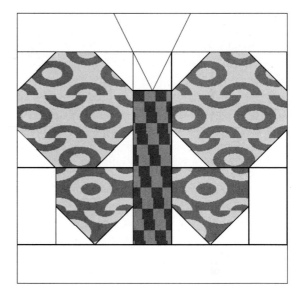

Piecing Diagram

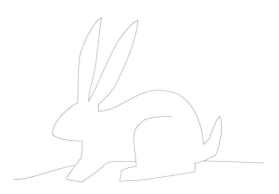

PIG

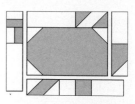

1½" finished square
8" x 11" block with seam allowance

Cut for one block:

1.	1 pig	5" x 8"	rectangle
2.	2 background	2" x 5"	rectangle
3.	3 background and 2 pig	2" x 3½"	rectangle
4.	1 background and 1 pig	1¼" x 5"	strip
5.	7 background and 3 pig	2"	square

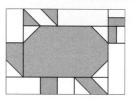

Piecing Diagram

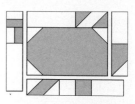

Reverse Pig Block

Directions:

1. Place a background 2" square on one end of a pig 2" x 3½" rectangle and sew a diagonal seam as shown. Outside the stitching, trim fabric to a ¼" seam. Press to the rectangle. (Reverse this piece for the reverse Pig block.)

2. Place a background 2" square on one end of a pig 2" x 3½" rectangle and sew a diagonal seam as shown. Trim and press. Place a background square on the other end. Sew the same diagonal, trim and press. *(This unit does have a reverse, so be sure to sew the correct diagonal.)* Make another one of these with the values reversed.

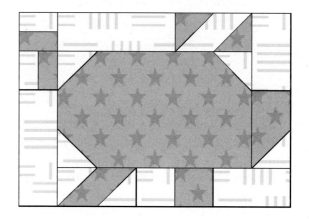

3. Sew the background and pig 1¼" x 5" strips together lengthwise. Press to the dark. Then cut two 2" sections from this strip set for the pig's tail.

4. Sew background 2" squares on three corners of the 5" x 8" pig rectangle with diagonal seams as shown. Trim and press. Assemble according to the piecing diagram.

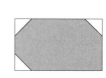

PIGLET

Cut for one block:

1.	1 piglet	5" x 8"	rectangle
2.	1 background	3½" x 5"	rectangle
3.	1 background	2" x 6½"	rectangle
4.	1 background	2" x 5"	rectangle
5.	2 background and 3 piglet	2" x 3½"	rectangle
6.	1 background and 1 piglet	1¼" x 5"	strip
7.	11 background and 2 piglet	2"	square

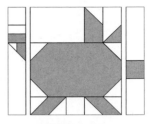

Piecing Diagram

Directions:

1. Place a background 2" square on one end of a piglet 2" x 3½" rectangle and sew a diagonal seam as shown. (A) Outside the stitching, trim fabric to a ¼" seam. Press to the rectangle. Make 2 of these. Take one of these and place a background square on the other end. Sew the same diagonal, trim and press. Make one with the diagonals in the other direction. Place a piglet 2" square on one end of a background 2" x 3½" rectangle and sew a diagonal seam as shown. (B) Trim and press.

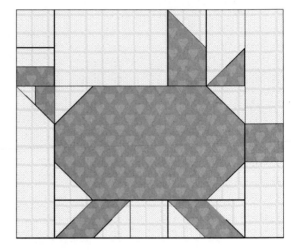

2. Sew background and piglet 1¼" x 5" strips together lengthwise. Press to the dark. Cut two 2" sections from this strip set. Take one section and place it on the end of a 2" x 6½" background rectangle. Sew a diagonal seam as shown, trim and press to the background.

3. Place four background 2" squares on all four corners of the 5" x 8" piglet rectangle and sew diagonally as shown. Trim and press to the rectangle. Assemble according to the piecing diagram.

11

 **CAT**

Cut for one block:

1.	2 cat	5" x 6½"	rectangle
2.	1 background and 1 cat	3⅞"	square
3.	1 background	3½" x 6½"	rectangle
4.	1 cat	3½"	square
5.	1 background	2" x 5"	rectangle
6.	2 cat	2" x 3½"	rectangle
7.	1 background and 1 cat	1¼" x 3½"	rectangle
8.	3 background 2 cat	2"	square

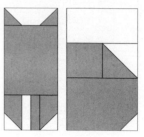

Piecing Diagram

Directions:

1. Cut one background and one cat 3⅞" square in half diagonally. Sew one of each together to make the cat's back. You will have one of each left for another block.

2. Sew the 1¼" x 3½" background and cat rectangles together lengthwise for part of the cat's paws.

3. Place a 2" background square on the lower right corner of a 5" x 6½" cat rectangle. Sew diagonally as shown. Trim outside the stitching to a ¼" seam. Press.

4. Place a background 2" square on one end of a cat 2" x 3½" rectangle. Sew diagonally, trim and press. Make one with the opposite diagonal. Place a cat 2" square on one end of the 2" x 5" background rectangle. Sew diagonally, trim and press. Place another cat 2" square on the other end and sew the opposite diagonal. Assemble according to the piecing diagram.

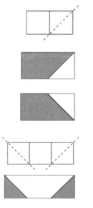

12

Cut for one block:

1.	1 background and 1 kitten	3⅞"	square
2.	2 kitten	3½" x 5"	rectangle
3.	1 background	3½"	square
4.	4 background and 1 kitten	2" x 3½"	rectangle
5.	1 background and 1 kitten	1¼" x 3½"	rectangle
6.	1 background and 2 kitten	2"	square

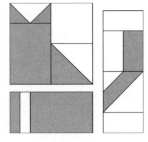

Piecing Diagram

Directions:

1. Place a background and a kitten 3⅞" square right sides together. Draw a corner to corner diagonal line on the back of the lightest of these. Sew ¼" away on both sides of the drawn line. Cut on the line. This produces two 3½" half-squares. Use one for the kitten's back. Place a background 2" square on the kitten corner of the other 3½" half-square. Sew diagonally, trim, and press to the dark (part of tail).

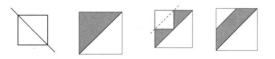

2. Sew the background and kitten 1¼" x 3½" rect-angles together lengthwise to make the kitten leg.

3. Place a kitten 2" square on one end of a back-ground 2" x 3½" rectangle. Sew diagonally. Trim outside the stitching to a ¼" seam allowance. Place a 2" kitten square on the other end. Sew the opposite diagonal. Trim and press (kitten ears). Assemble according to the piecing diagram.

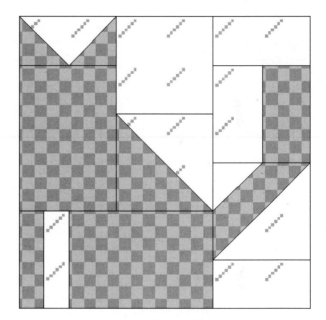

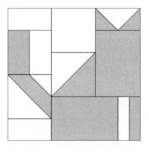

Reverse Kitten Block

HEN

Cut for one block:

1.	1 medium and 1 dark	3⅞"	square
2.	1 background	3½" x 8"	rectangle
3.	1 background	3½" x 5"	rectangle
4.	1 background	2" x 9½"	rectangle
5.	1 medium	2" x 6½"	rectangle
6.	2 background	2" x 5"	rectangle
7.	2 background and 2 medium	2" x 3½"	rectangle
8.	1 background and 1 medium	1¼" x 5½"	strip
9.	3 background and 7 medium	2"	square

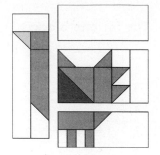

Piecing Diagram

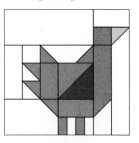

Reverse Hen Block

Directions:

1. Sew the background and medium 1¼" x 5½" strips together lengthwise. Press to the dark. Then cut two 2" sections from this set of strips for chicken feet.

2. (A) Place a medium 2" square on the upper left corner of the 3½" x 5" background rectangle and sew a diagonal seam as shown. Outside the stitching, trim fabric to a ¼" seam. Press to the rectangle. (B) Place a medium 2" square on one end of a background 2" x 9½" rectangle and sew a diagonal seam as shown. Trim and press to the rectangle. (C) Place a medium square on one end of a 2" x 5" background rectangle. Sew diagonally as shown, trim and press. Place a medium square on the other end. Sew the opposite diagonal, trim and press. (D) Place a background 2" x 3½" rectangle on one end of the medium 2" x 6½" rectangle on the perpendicular as shown. Sew diagonally, trim and press.

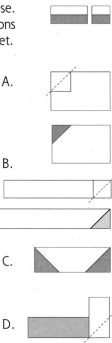

A.

B.

C.

D.

3. Cut the medium and dark 3⅞" squares in half diagonally. Sew one of each together to make a large half-square (chicken wing). You will have one of each left over for another block.

4. Place a medium and background 2" square right sides together and sew a diagonal seam. Trim one side to a ¼" seam. Open and press to the dark. Make 2 of these. This is a half-square. Assemble according to the piecing diagram.

ROOSTER

Cut for one block:

1.	1 rooster and 1 dark	3⅞"	square
2.	1 background	3½" x 5"	rectangle
3.	1 background	2" x 9½"	rectangle
4.	2 rooster	2" x 5"	rectangle
5.	2 background, 3 rooster, and 2 dark	2" x 3½"	rectangle
6.	3 background, 2 rooster, 2 beak, and 1 dark*	1¼" x 2"	rectangle
7.	8 background, 10 rooster, and 1 beak	2"	square

Or cut longer ¼" pieces , sew them together lengthwise, and then trim to 2".

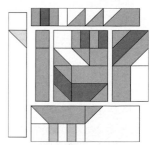

Piecing Diagram

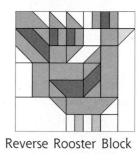

Reverse Rooster Block

Directions:

1. Cut one rooster and one dark 3⅞" square diagonally as shown. Sew one background and one dark of the resulting triangles together to make the rooster's tail. (You will have one of each left over for another block.) Place a background 2" square on the rooster corner of this 3½" half-square. Sew diagonally, trim, and press to the dark. Place a rooster 2" square on the dark corner and sew diagonally again. Trim and press.

2. Sew the 1¼" x 2" rectangles together in the combinations shown in the block diagram. *See Note* above.* (feet, comb and tail)

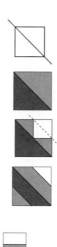

3. (A) Place a beak 2" square on one end of the background 2" x 9½" rectangle and sew a diagonal seam as shown. Outside the stitching, trim fabric to a ¼" seam. Press to the beak. (B) Place a background 2" square on one end of the rooster 2" x 5" rectangle and sew a diagonal seam as shown. (C) Place a rooster 2" square on one end of a dark 2" x 3½" rectangle and sew a diagonal seam as shown. Make two of these. Take one and place a rooster square on the other end. Sew the same diagonal, trim and press. (D) Make one rooster-background unit as shown.

A.

B.

C.

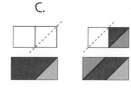

D.

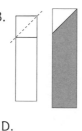

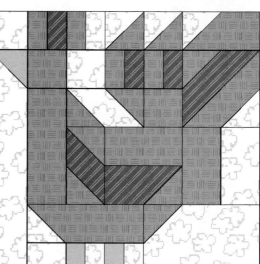

4. Place a rooster square on one corner of the background 3½" x 5" rectangle as shown. Sew a diagonal seam.

5. Place a background and rooster 2" square right sides together. Sew a diagonal seam. Trim one side to ¼" seam allowance. Press to the dark. Make two of these. Assemble according to the piecing diagram.

LITTLE SQUIRREL

1½" finished square
9½" block with seam allowance

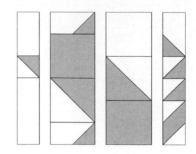

Cut for one block:

1.	1 background and 1 squirrel	3⅞"	square
2.	1 background and 2 squirrel	3½"	square
3.	1 background	2" x 5"	rectangle
4.	4 background and 1 squirrel	2" x 3½"	rectangle
5.	5 background and 6 squirrel	2"	square

Piecing Diagram

Directions:

1. Cut one squirrel and one background 3⅞" square in half diagonally. Sew one each of the resulting background and squirrel triangles together to make the squirrel body. This is a 3½" half-square. Make two of these.

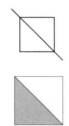

2. (A) Place a squirrel 2" square on one end of a background 2" x 3½" rectangle. Sew a diagonal seam as shown. Trim outside the stitching to a ¼" seam allowance and press to the dark. Make three. (B) Place a background 2" square on one end of a squirrel 2" x 3½" rectangle. Sew diagonally as shown, trim and press. Place another background 2" square at the other end. Sew the same diagonal, trim and press. *(This piece does have a reverse, so be sure to sew the correct diagonal.)*

A.

B.

3. Place a background and squirrel 2" square right sides together. Sew together with a diagonal line. Trim away excess fabric on one side of the stitched line to leave a ¼" seam. Press to the dark. Make three of these. This is a 2" half-square. Assemble according to the piecing diagram.

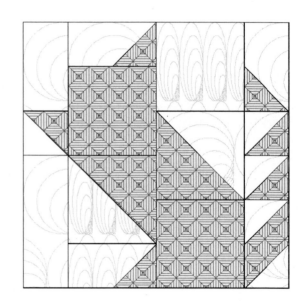

BIG SQUIRREL

1 ½" finished square
11" block with seam allowance

Cut for one block:

1.	1 background and 1 squirrel	5⅜"	square
2.	1 background and 1 squirrel	3⅞"	square
3.	1 squirrel	5"	square
4.	1 background	2" x 8"	rectangle
5.	1 background and 2 squirrel	2" x 5"	rectangle
6.	1 background and 2 squirrel	2" x 3½"	rectangle
7.	7 background and 4 squirrel	2"	square

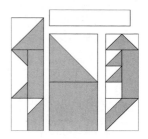

Piecing Diagram

Directions:

1. (A) Cut one squirrel and one background 5⅜" square in half diagonally. Sew together one of each resulting triangle to make the squirrel back. You will have one of each left over for another block. (B) Cut the background and squirrel 3⅞" squares in half diagonally as shown. Sew one of each of the resulting triangles together to make a large half-square. Make two of these. Place a background 2" square on the squirrel corner of one 3½" half-square. Sew diagonally, trim, and press to the squirrel fabric.

A.

B.

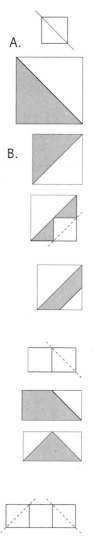

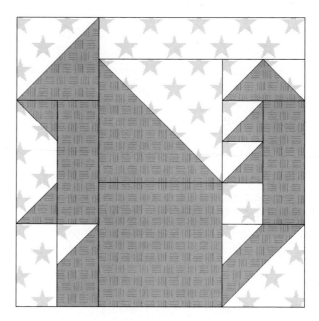

2. Place a background 2" square on one end of a squirrel 2" x 3½" rectangle and sew a diagonal seam as shown. Outside the stitching, trim fabric to a ¼" seam. Press to the dark. Make two. Take one of these and place a background square on the other end. Sew the opposite diagonal, trim and press.

3. Place a squirrel 2" square on one end of a background 2" x 5" rectangle and sew a diagonal seam as shown. Trim and press. Place a squirrel square on the other end. Sew the opposite diagonal, trim and press.

5. Place a background and squirrel 2" square right sides together and sew a diagonal seam. Trim one side to a ¼" seam allowance and press to the dark. Make two of these. This is a 2" half-square. Assemble according to the piecing diagram.

REINDEER

Cut for one block:

1.	1 background	5"	square
2.	1 reindeer	3½" x 6½"	rectangle
3.	1 background	2" x 9½"	rectangle
4.	1 background	2" x 5"	rectangle
5.	2 background and 2 reindeer	2" x 3½"	rectangle
6.	1 background and 1 reindeer	1¼"	strip
7.	2 background and 4 reindeer	2"	square

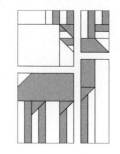

Piecing Diagram

Directions:

1. Sew the background and reindeer 1¼" strips together lengthwise. Press to the dark. Then cut the following sections from this set of strips:

1.	3	5"	section
2.	1	6½"	section
3.	1	3½"	section
4.	6	2"	section

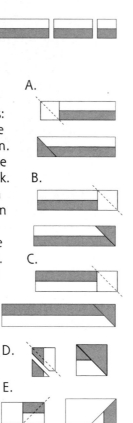

2. Finish the strip sections as follows:
(A) Place a reindeer 2" square on one end of a 5" strip section as shown. Sew a diagonal seam according to the diagram. Trim and press to the dark.
(B) Place a reindeer 2" square on the other end of a 5" strip section as shown. Sew the same diagonal.
(C) Sew a reindeer 2" square on one end of the 6½" strip section as shown.
(D) Sew a reindeer square right sides together with a 2" strip section as shown. Press to the square.
(E) Place a 2" strip section on one end of a background 2" x 3½" rectangle as shown and sew a diagonal seam according to the diagram. Trim and press to the background.

A.

B.

C.

D.

E.

3. Place a background 2" square on one end of a reindeer 2" x 3½" rectangle and sew a diagonal seam as shown. Outside the stitching, trim fabric to a ¼" seam. Press to the dark (head).

4. Sew a background 2" square on one corner of the 3½" x 6½" reindeer rectangle using a diagonal seam as shown. Trim and press. Assemble according to the piecing diagram.

 FAWN

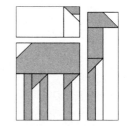

1½" finished square
9½" x 11" block with seam allowance

Cut #2, 3, and 4 as for reindeer, pg. 18, then cut for one block:

1.	1 background	3½" x 5"	rectangle
5.	1 background and 2 reindeer	2" x 3½"	rectangle
6.	1 background and 1 reindeer	1¼"	strip
7.	2 background and 3 reindeer	2"	square

Piecing Diagram

Directions:

1. Sew the background and reindeer 1¼" strips together lengthwise. Press to the dark. Then cut the following sections from this set of strips:

1.	3	5"	section
2.	1	6½"	section
3.	1	2"	section

2. Make (A), (B), (C), and (E) as in Reindeer block on pg. 18. Then assemble as a Reindeer block without antlers, according to the piecing diagram. This is a Fawn block.

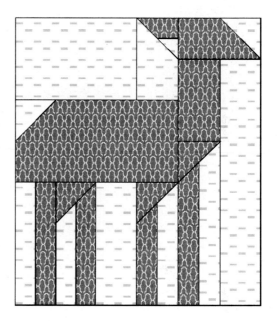

**DEER**

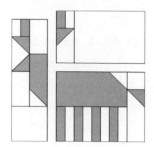
Cut for one block:

1.	1 background	5" x 6½"	rectangle
2.	1 deer	3½" x 6½"	rectangle
3.	1 background	3½"	square
4.	1 background and 1 deer	2" x 5"	rectangle
5.	4 background	2" x 3½"	rectangle
6.	1 background and 1 deer	1¼" x 20"	strip
7.	3 background and 4 deer	2"	square

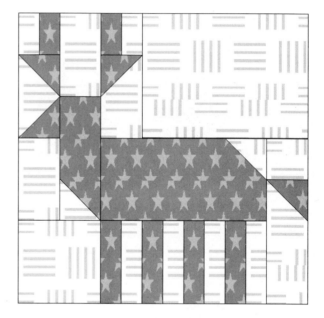

Piecing Diagram

Directions:

1. Sew the background and deer 1¼" strips together lengthwise. Press to the dark. Then cut the following sections from this set of strips:

1.	4	3½" section
2.	2	2" section

2. (A) Place a deer 2" square on one end of a background 2" x 3½" rectangle and sew a diagonal seam as shown. Outside the stitching, trim fabric to a ¼" seam. Press. Make two of these. Take one of these and place a background square on the other end. Sew the opposite diagonal, trim and press. (B) Place a deer 2" square on one end of a background 2" x 5" rectangle and sew a diagonal seam as shown. Trim and press. Make another one of these with values reversed.

A.

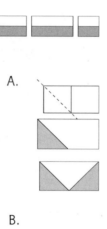

B.

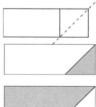

3. Sew one background 2" square onto the upper right corner of a deer 3½" x 6½" with a diagonal seam as shown. Trim and press. Assemble according to the piecing diagram.

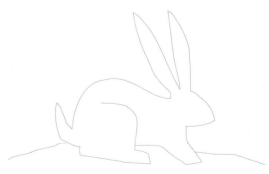

MOOSE

1½" finished square
12½" block with seam allowance

Cut for one block:

1.	1 moose	6½" x 8"	rectangle
2.	1 background and 1 moose	3½" x 5"	rectangle
3.	5 background and 4 moose	3½" x 2"	rectangle
4.	1 background and 1 moose	2" x 9"	strip
5.	11 background and 8 moose	2"	square

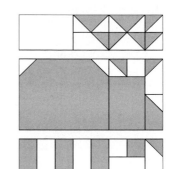

Directions:

1. Sew the background and moose 2" x 9" strips together lengthwise. This strip set will be 3½" wide. Then cut one 2" length and two 3½" lengths from this strip set.

2. (A) Place a moose 2" square at one end of a background 3½" x 2" rectangle and sew a diagonal seam as shown. Trim outside the stitching to a ¼" seam and press. Make three of these. (B) Make one with the diagonal in the other direction and set aside. (C) Make three with values reversed as shown. (D) Place a background 2" square on the other end of a moose unit (C) above. Sew the opposite diagonal. Trim and press. Make two of these. Make one with values reversed as shown.

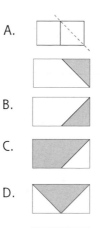

A.

B.

C.

D.

3. Place a background and moose 2" square right sides together. Sew a diagonal seam, trim one side to ¼" and press to the dark. Make three. This is a 2" half-square.

4. Place a background 2" square on one corner of the moose 6½" x 8" rectangle. Sew the diagonal, trim, and press. Place a background 2" square on the other end of the long side, sew, trim, and press. Assemble according to the piecing diagram.

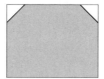

Piecing Diagram

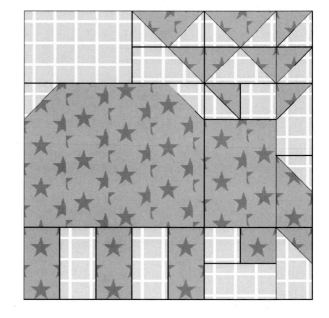

21

BULL ELEPHANT

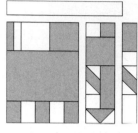

Cut for one block:

1.	1 elephant	5¾" x 8"	rectangle
2.	1 background and 2 elephant	3½"	square
3.	1 background	2" x 12½"	rectangle
4.	1 background and 1 elephant	2" x 8"	strip
5.	1 elephant	2" x 5"	rectangle
6.	1 background and 4 elephant	2" x 3½"	rectangle
7.	1 elephant	2" x 2¾"	rectangle
8.	1 background and 1 elephant	1¼" x 3½"	strip
9.	8 background	2"	square

Piecing Diagram

Directions:

1. Sew the background and elephant 2" x 8" strips together lengthwise. Cut from this set of strips:

1.	2	2¾"	leg section
2.	1	2"	ear section

2. Sew the background and elephant 1¼" strips together for the elephant tail.

3. (A) Place a background 2" square on one end of an elephant 2" x 3½" rectangle and sew a diagonal seam as shown. Outside the stitching, trim fabric to a ¼" seam. Press to the dark. Make three of these. (B) Place a background square on the other end of (A). Sew the same diagonal, trim and press. Make two of these. (C) Place a background 2" square on the other end the of the remaining (A). Sew the opposite diagonal. Trim and press. Assemble according to the piecing diagram.

A.

B.

C.

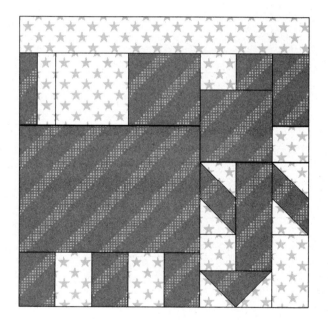

ELEPHANT

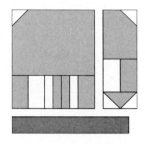
Cut for one block:

1.	1 elephant	6½" x 8"	rectangle
2.	1 elephant	3½" x 5"	rectangle
3.	1 dark*	2" x 11"	rectangle
4.	1 background and 1 elephant	2" x 7"	strip
5.	2 elephant	2" x 3½"	rectangle
6.	1 background and 1 elephant	1¼" x 7"	strip
7.	4 background	2"	square

Do not cut this strip when making a block for the Animal Sampler Quilt.

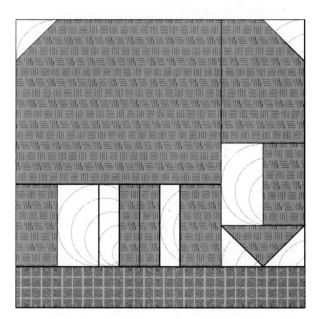

Piecing Diagram

Directions:

1. Sew the background and elephant 2" x 7" strips together lengthwise. Press to the dark. Sew the background and elephant 1¼" strips together lengthwise. Press to the dark. Then cut two 3½" sections from both sets of strips:

2. (A) Place a background 2" square on one end of an elephant 2" x 3½" rectangle and sew a diagonal seam as shown. Outside the stitching, trim fabric to a ¼" seam. Press to the dark. Then place another background square on the other end. Sew the opposite diagonal, trim and press. (B) Sew a background 2" square on one corner of the 3½" x 5" elephant rectangle with a diagonal seam as shown. Trim and press to the dark. (C) Sew a background 2" square on one corner of the 6½" x 8" elephant rectangle with a diagonal seam as shown. Trim and press. Assemble according to the piecing diagram.

A.

B.

C.

LITTLE BIRD

1½" finished square
9½" block with seam allowance

Cut for one block:

1.	1 background	3½" x 5"	rectangle
2.	3 background	3½"	square
3.	1 background and 2 bird	3½" x 2"	rectangle
4.	1 background and 1 bird	3½" x 1¼"	rectangle
5.	1 bird	2" x 9½"	rectangle
6.	4 background and 6 bird	2"	square

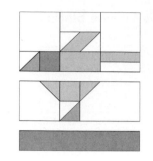

Piecing Diagram

Directions:

1. (A) Place a background 2" square on the right end of a bird 3½" x 2" rectangle. Sew diagonally as shown. Trim outside the stitching to a ¼" seam. Press to the dark. Place another background 2" square on the other end of the bird rectangle and sew the same diagonal. Trim and press again. *(Note, this piece does have an opposite, so check to be sure the diagonals are correct.)* (B) Place a bird 2" square on one corner of a 3½" background square. Sew diagonally across the corner, trim and press to the background. (C) Place a bird 2" square on one corner of a 3½" x 5" background rectangle. Sew diagonally, trim and press to the background.

A.

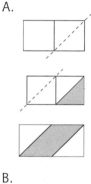

B.

C.

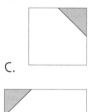

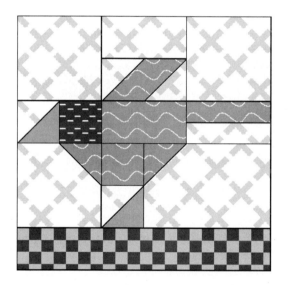

2. Place a background and bird square together and sew diagonally. Trim one side to a ¼" seam allowance and press the seam to the dark. Make two of these. This is a 2" half-square.

3. Sew the background and bird 3½" x 1¼" rectangles together lengthwise. Assemble all the pieces according to the piecing diagram.

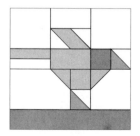

Reverse Block

OSTRICH

Cut for one block:

1.	1 background	5" x 6½"	rectangle
2.	1 background and 1 ostrich	5"	square
3.	1 background	3½" x 5"	rectangle
4.	1 background	2" x 9½"	rectangle
5.	1 background and 1 ostrich	2" x 3½"	rectangle
6.	1 background and 1 ostrich	1¼" x 12"	strip
7.	7 background and 7 ostrich	2"	square

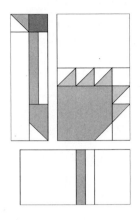

Piecing Diagram

Directions:

1. Sew the background and ostrich 1¼" strips together lengthwise. Press to the dark. Then cut a 5" section and a 6½" section from this set of strips.

2. (A) Place an ostrich 2" square on one end of a background 2" x 3½" rectangle and sew a diagonal seam as shown. Outside the stitching, trim fabric to a ¼" seam. Press to the dark. (B) Place a background 2" square on one end of an ostrich 2" x 3½" rectangle and sew a diagonal seam as shown. Trim and press to the dark. (C) Place a background 2" square on one corner of the 5" ostrich square. Sew a diagonal seam as shown, trim and press.

A.

B.

C.

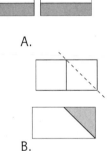

3. Place a background and ostrich 2" square right sides together and sew a diagonal seam. Trim on one side of the stitching to a ¼" seam allowance. Press to the dark. Make five of these. This is a 2" half-square. Assemble according to the piecing diagram.

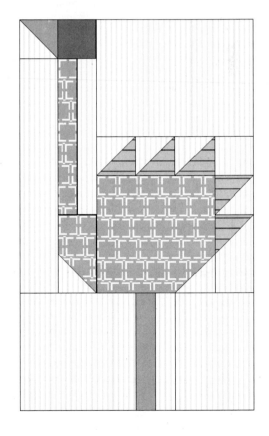

GIRAFFE

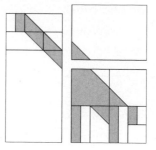
Cut for one block:

1.	1 background	5" x 8"	rectangle
2.	1 background	5" x 6½"	rectangle
3.	1 background and 1 giraffe	3½"	square
4.	3 background	3½" x 2"	rectangle
5.	1 background and 1 giraffe	1¼" x 12"	strip
6.	3 background and 7 giraffe	2"	square

Piecing Diagram

Directions:

1. Sew the background and giraffe 1¼" x 12" strips together lengthwise. (The strip set will be 2" wide.) From this strip set cut two 2" and two 3½" sections.

2. (A) Place a giraffe 2" square on one end of a 3½" x 2" background rectangle. Sew diagonally as shown. Trim outside the stitching to a ¼" seam and press to the dark. Make two of these. Make another one with the diagonal going the other way. (B) Sew a giraffe 2" square diagonally on one corner of a background 3½" square. (C) Sew a background 2" square diagonally on one corner of a giraffe 3½" square as shown. (D) Sew a giraffe 2" square diagonally on the lower left corner of a 5" x 6½" background rectangle as shown. (E) Sew a giraffe 2" square diagonally on the upper right corner of a background 5" x 8" rectangle.

A.

B.

C.

D.   E.

3. Place a background and giraffe 2" square right sides together. Sew diagonally, trim and press. This is a 2" half-square. Assemble according to the piecing diagram.

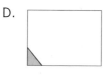

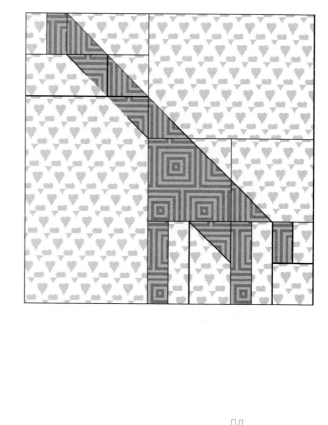

ZEBRA/HORSE

Cut for one block:

1.	1 zebra	5" x 8"	rectangle
2.	1 background and 1 zebra	3⅞"	square
3.	1 zebra	3½"	square
4.	1 background	2" x 5"	rectangle
5.	2 background and 1 zebra	2" x 3½"	rectangle
6.	1 background and 1 zebra	1¼"	strip
7.	2 background and 1 zebra	2"	square

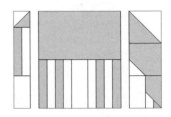

Piecing Diagram

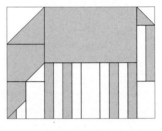

Reverse Zebra Block

Directions:

1. Sew the background and zebra 1¼" strips together lengthwise. Press to the dark. Then cut the following sections from this set of strips:

1.	5	5" section
2.	1	2" section

2. Cut one background and one zebra 3⅞" square in half diagonally. Then sew one of each of the resulting triangles together as shown (neck). *(You will have one of each triangle left for another block.)*

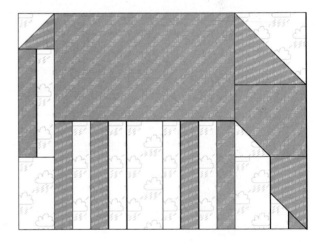

3. (A) Place a background 2" square on one corner of the zebra 3½" square and sew a diagonal seam as shown. Outside the stitching, trim fabric to a ¼" seam. Press to the dark. (B) Place the 2" strip section on one end of a zebra 2" x 3½" rectangle according to the diagram and sew diagonally as shown. Trim and press to the dark. *Make a reverse head for a reverse Zebra/Horse block.*

Reverse

A.

B.

4. Place a background and zebra 2" square right sides together and sew a diagonal seam. Trim the excess fabric from one side to leave a ¼" seam allowance. Press to the dark. This is a 2" half-square. Assemble according to the piecing diagram.

DOG

Cut for one block:

1.	1 background and 1 dog	5" x 6½"	rectangle
2.	1 dog	3½"	square
3.	1 background*	2" x 12½"	rectangle
4.	1 background and 1 dog	2" x 12"	strip
5.	1 background	2" x 6½"	rectangle
6.	1 background and 3 dog	2" x 3½"	rectangle
7.	1 background and 1 dog	1¼" x 10"	strip
8.	2 background and 5 dog	2"	square

* Do not cut this background strip when piecing a block for the Noah's Ark quilt.

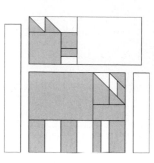

Piecing Diagram

Directions:

1. Sew the background and dog 2" strips together lengthwise. Press to the dark. Then cut two 3½" sections from this set of strips. Sew the background and dog 1¼" strips together lengthwise. Press to the dark. Then cut sections from this set of strips:

1.	2	3½" section
2.	1	2" section

2. (A) Take one of the 3½" sections of the 1¼" strip set and place a dog 2" square on one end according to the diagram. Sew a diagonal seam as shown. Outside the stitching, trim fabric to a ¼" seam. Press to the square. Place another dog square on the other end and sew the same diagonal, trim and press. (B) Place a dog 2" square on one end of a background 2" x 3½" rectangle and sew a diagonal seam as shown. Trim and press to the square. (C) Place a background 2" square on one end of a dog 2" x 3½" rectangle and sew a diagonal seam as shown. Trim and press.

A.

B.

C.

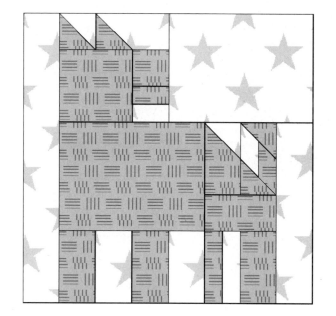

3. Place a background and dog 2" square right sides together and sew a diagonal seam. Trim on one side of the stitching to a ¼" seam allowance. Press to the dark. This is a half-square. Assemble according to the piecing diagram.

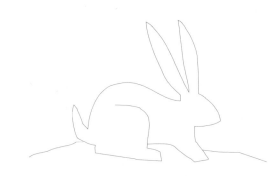

Fox

Cut for one block:

1.	1 fox	5" x 6½"	rectangle
2.	1 background and 1 fox	3⅞"	square
3.	1 background	3½" x 9½"	rectangle
4.	1 background and 1 fox	3½" x 6½"	rectangle
5.	1 background	3½" x 5"	rectangle
6.	1 background	3½"	square
7.	1 background and 1 fox	2" x 5"	rectangle
8.	2 background and 2 fox	2" x 3½"	rectangle
9.	4 background, 5 fox and 1 tail fabric	2"	square

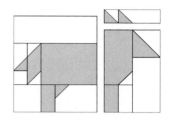

Piecing Diagram

Directions:

1. Make these pieces:
(A) Place a fox 2" square on one end of a background 2" x 3½" rectangle and sew a diagonal seam as shown. Outside the stitching, trim fabric to a ¼" seam. Press to the dark. (B) Place a background 2" square on one end of a fox 2" x 5" rectangle and sew a diagonal seam as shown. Trim and press. Place a background square on the other end. Sew the same diagonal, trim and press. (C) Place a fox 2" square on one end of a background 2" x 5" rectangle and sew a diagonal seam as shown. Trim and press. (D) Sew a background 2" square on one corner of the fox 3½" x 6½" rectangle with a diagonal seam as shown. Trim and press to the dark. (E) Sew a fox 2" square on one corner of the 3½" x 5" background rectangle with a diagonal seam as shown. Trim and press to the dark.

A.

B.

C.

D.

E.

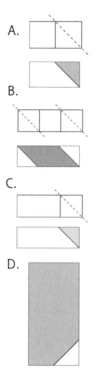

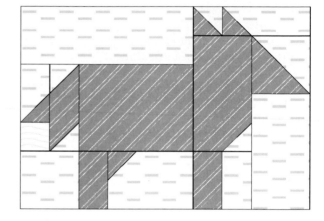

2. Cut the background and fox 3⅞" squares in half diagonally as shown. Sew one of each of the resulting triangles together to make a large half-square. *(You will have one of each left over for another block.)*

3. Place a background and fox 2" square right sides together and sew a diagonal seam. Trim on one side of the stitching to a ¼" seam allowance. Press to the dark. This is a 2" half-square. Assemble according to the piecing diagram.

DUCK

Cut for one block:

1.	1 background	5" x 6½"	rectangle
2.	2 background and 2 dark	3⅞"	square
3.	1 medium	3½"	square
4.	1 medium	3½" x 5"	rectangle
5.	1 dark	2" x 8"	rectangle
6.	1 dark	2" x 5"	rectangle
7.	1 background, 1 medium and 2 dark	2" x 3½"	rectangle
8.	1 background and 1 medium	1¼" x 3½"	strip
9.	5 background, 1 medium and 1 dark	2"	square

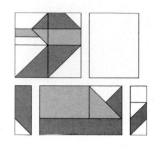

Piecing Diagram

Directions:

1. (A) Cut the background and dark 3⅞" squares in half diagonally. Sew the resulting background and dark triangles together to make three units as shown. *(You will have one of each triangle left for another block.)*
(B) Place one of the background-dark half-squares (should measure 3½") right sides together with the medium 3½" square as shown and sew a diagonal seam according to the diagram. Trim to a ¼" seam.

A.

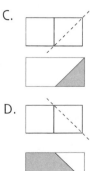

B.

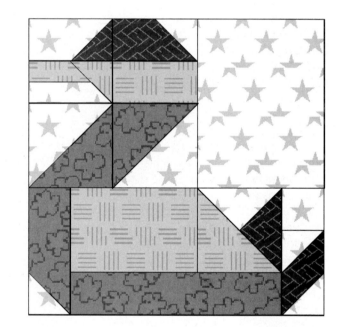

2. (C) Place a dark 2" square on one end of a background 2" x 3½" rectangle and sew a diagonal seam as shown. Outside the stitching, trim fabric to a ¼" seam. Press to the dark. (D) Place a background 2" square on one end of a dark 2" x 3½" rectangle and sew a diagonal seam as shown. Trim and press to the dark. Make two of these. Take one of these and place a background square on the other end. Sew the same diagonal, trim and press.

C.

D.

3. Place a background 2" square on one end of a dark 2" x 5" rectangle and sew a diagonal seam as shown. Trim and press.

4. Sew the background and medium 1¼" strips together lengthwise. Place a medium 2" square on one end according to the diagram. Sew a diagonal seam as shown, trim, and press to the triangle. Assemble according to the piecing diagram.

Cut for one block:

1.	2 owl, I background and 1 wing	3⅞"	square
2.	1 owl and 1 wing	3½" x 6½"	rectangle
3.	1 owl	3½" x 5"	rectangle
4.	1 background and 1 wing	3½"	square
5.	1 owl	2" x 8"	rectangle
6.	1 background	2" x 5"	rectangle
7.	1 owl, 1 background and 1 foot	2" x 3½"	rectangle
8.	4 owl, 5 background, 1 beak and 1 foot	2"	square

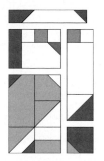

Piecing Diagram

Directions:

1. Cut the owl, wing, and background 3⅞" squares in half diagonally as shown. Sew the resulting triangles together to make three large half-squares in the combinations shown in the chart below.

Make 2

Make 1

1.	2	wing/owl triangle
2.	1	owl/background triangle

2. Take one of the wing/owl half-squares and place a background 2" square on the owl corner of this 3½" half-square as shown. Sew diagonally as in the diagram. Outside the stitching, trim fabric to a ¼" seam allowance, and press to the dark.

3. (A) Place a 2" square of owl foot fabric on one corner of a background 3½" square and sew a diagonal seam as shown. (B) Make one with a 2" owl square and a 3½" wing square. Trim and press. (C) Place a background 2" square on the left upper corner of a wing 3½" x 6½" rectangle and sew diagonally as shown. (D) Place an owl beak 2" square on the upper right corner of the 3½" x 5" owl rectangle and sew a diagonal seam as shown.

A.

B.

C.

D.

(E) Place a background 2" square on the right end of the owl 2" x 8" rectangle and sew a diagonal seam as shown. Then place a 2" x 3½" background rectangle perpendicular to the left end of the owl 2" x 8" rectangle and sew diagonally as shown. (use the opposite diagonal) Trim and press to the dark. Assemble according to the piecing diagram.

E.

BUNNY

1½" each finished square
11" each block with seam allowance

Cut for one block:

1.	1 bunny	5" x 8"	rectangle
2.	1 background	5" x 6½"	rectangle
3.	1 background and 1 bunny	3⅞"	square
4.	1 background	3½"	square
5.	1 background and 1 bunny	2" x 5"	rectangle
6.	1 background and 2 bunny	2" x 3½"	rectangle
7.	9 background and 4 bunny	2"	square

Directions:

1. Cut the background and bunny 3⅞" squares in half diagonally as shown. Sew one of each of the resulting triangles together to make a large half-square. (You will have one of each triangle left over for another block.) Place a background 2" square on the bunny corner of this 3½" half-square. Sew diagonally, trim, and press to the bunny fabric.

2. Make these pieces:

(A) Place a bunny square over the right end of a background 2" x 3½" rectangle, right sides together. Sew a diagonal seam as shown. Trim and press to the triangle.

A.

(B) Place a background square over one end of a 2" x 3½" bunny rectangle, right sides together. Sew a diagonal line. Trim and press to the triangle. Make two of these.

B. Make two

(C) Place another background square at the other end of one of (B). Sew the **opposite** diagonal. Trim and press.

C.

(D) Place another background square at the other end of one of (B). Sew the **same** diagonal. Trim and press. (Be sure the diagonal is going in the right direction, it does have a reverse.)

D.

(E) Place a bunny 2" square on two adjacent corners of the 3½" background square as shown. Sew diagonally, trim and press.

E.

(F) Sew a background 2" square on both ends of a 2" x 5" bunny rectangle, sewing the same diagonal at both ends as shown. (Be sure the diagonal is going in the right direction, it does have a reverse.)

F.

(G) Place a background square at the upper right corner of the 5" x 8" dark rectangle, right sides together. Sew the diagonal seam, trim and press. Assemble into a block as shown by the piecing diagram.

G.

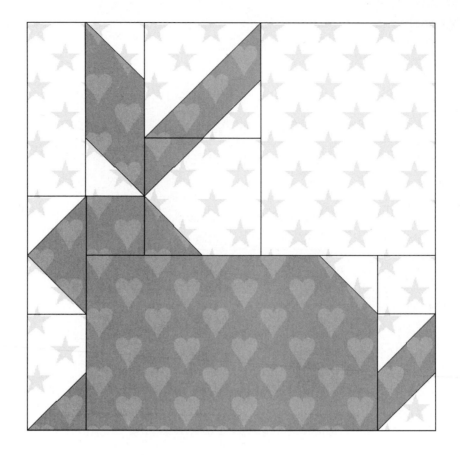

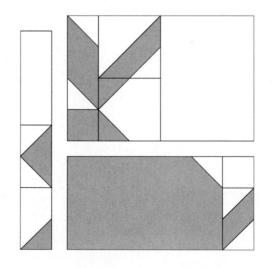

Piecing Diagram

COW

1½" finished square
9½" x 15½" block with seam allowance

Cut for one block:

1.	1 cow	5" x 9½"	rectangle
2.	1 background and 1 cow	3⅞"	square
3.	2 background	2" x 5"	rectangle
4.	1 cow	2" x 4¼"	rectangle
5.	2 background and 1 cow	2" x 3½"	rectangle
6.	1 background and 1 cow	1¼"	strip
7.	3 background and 5 cow	2"	square
8.	1 background	1¼" x 2"	rectangle
9.	1 background	1¼"	square

Directions:

1. Sew the background and cow 1¼" strips together lengthwise. Press to the dark. Then cut the following sections from this set of strips:

1.	4	5" section
2.	1	3½" section
3.	3	2" section

2. Place a cow 2" square on one end of a 5" strip section as shown and sew a diagonal seam according to the diagram. Outside the stitching, trim fabric to a ¼" seam. Press to the square. Make 3 of these. Place a cow 2" square on one end of a 3½" strip section as shown and sew a diagonal seam according to the diagram. Trim and press to the square. (Reverse these pieces for the reverse Cow block.)

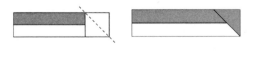

3. Cut the background and cow 3⅞" squares in half diagonally. Sew one of each of the resulting triangles together to make a large half-square as shown. Make two of these.

4. (A) Sew the background 1¼" square on one corner of the cow 2" x 4¼" rectangle with a diagonal seam as shown. Trim and press to the rectangle. (B) Sew a background 2" square on one corner of the cow 5" x 9½" rectangle as shown. Trim and press to the rectangle. (Reverse these pieces for the reverse block.)

A.   B.

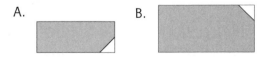

5. Place a background and cow 2" square right sides together and sew a diagonal seam. Trim on one side of the stitching to a ¼" seam allowance. Press to the dark. This is a half-square. Assemble according to the piecing diagram.

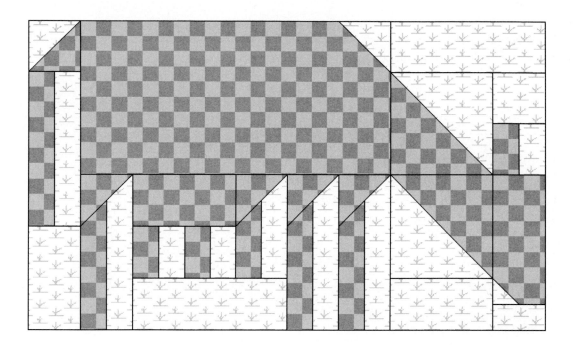

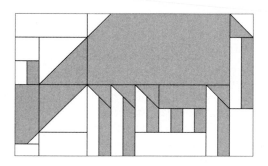

Reverse Cow Block

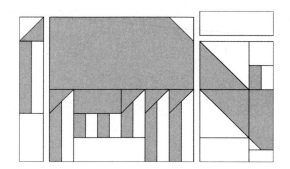

Piecing Diagram

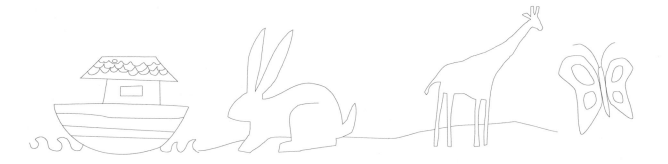

FLAMINGO

1½" finished square
11" x 15½" block with seam allowance

Cut for one block:

1.	1 background	6½"	square
2.	1 background	5"	square
3.	1 background and 1 flamingo	3⅞"	square
4.	1 background	3½" x 6½"	rectangle
5.	2 background and 1 flamingo	3½"	square
6.	1 background	2" x 4¼"	rectangle
7.	1 background	2" x 3½"	rectangle
8.	1 background and 1 flamingo	1¼" x 20"	strip
9.	1 flamingo	1¼" x 3½"	rectangle
10.	5 background and 6 flamingo	2"	square

Directions:

1. Sew the background and flamingo 1¼" strips together lengthwise. Press to the dark. Then cut these sections from the set of strips:

1.	1	5" section
2.	1	4¼" section
3.	4	2" section

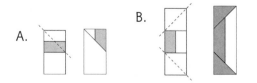

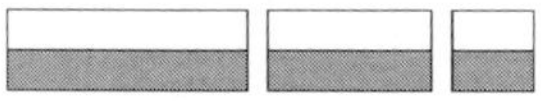

2. (A) Place a 2" strip set on one end of a background 2" x 3½" rectangle right sides together and sew a diagonal seam according to the diagram. Trim and press to the rectangle (beak). (B) Sew a background 2" square on both ends of the 5" strip section, using opposite diagonals (neck). Trim and press to the squares.

A.   B.

3. Place a background and flamingo 2" square right sides together and sew a diagonal seam. Trim away the fabric on one side of the stitching to leave a ¼" seam allowance. Press to the dark. This is a 2" half-square.

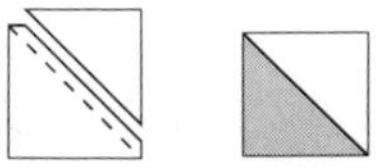

4. Place the background and flamingo 3⅞" squares right sides together. Draw a corner-to-corner diagonal line on the back of the light square. Sew a ¼" seam on both sides of this line. Cut sewn squares in half diagonally on the line as shown. Place a background 2" square on the flamingo corner of one of these 3½" half-squares. Sew diagonally, trim, and press to the flamingo fabric.

5. (C) Sew two flamingo squares on two adjacent corners of the 3½" background square as shown. Trim and press away from the small squares. (D) Sew two flamingo 2" squares on two adjacent corners as shown of the 5" background square. Assemble according to the piecing diagram.

C.   D.

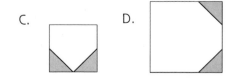

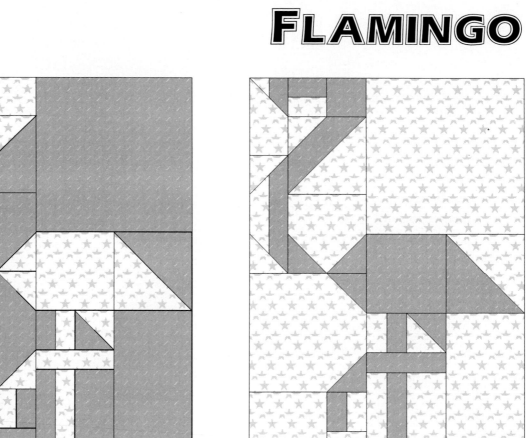

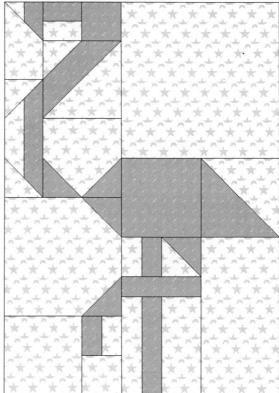

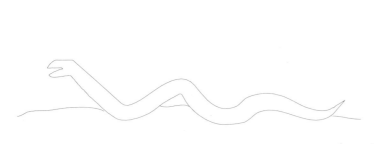

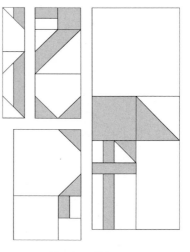

Piecing Diagram

 GOAT

1½" finished square
12½" block with seam allowance

Cut for one block:

1.	1 background and 1 goat	5" x 8"	rectangle
2.	2 background	3½" x 5"	rectangle
3.	1 background and 1 goat	2" x 5"	rectangle
4.	5 goat	2" x 3½"	rectangle
5.	1 background and 1 goat	1¼" x 8"	strip
6.	15 background and 4 goat	2"	square

Directions:

1. Sew the background and goat 1¼" strips together lengthwise. Press to the dark. Then cut the following sections from this set of strips:

1.	1	3½" section
2.	2	2" section

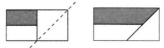

2. Place a background 2" square on one end of a 3½" strip section according to the diagram. Sew a diagonal seam as shown.

3. Place a background and goat 2" square right sides together. Sew a diagonal seam. Trim one side of the stitching to a ¼" seam, and press to the dark. This is a 2" half-square.

4. Place a background 2" square on one end of a goat 2" x 3½" rectangle and sew a diagonal seam as shown. Outside the stitching, trim fabric to a ¼" seam. Press to the dark. Make five. Set two aside.

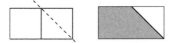

5. Take one of #4 and place a background square on the other end. Sew the opposite diagonal, trim and press. Make two of these. Place a background square on the other end of the remaining goat-background unit. Sew the same diagonal, trim and press.

6. Sew a background 2" square on one end of the goat 2" x 5" rectangle diagonally as shown.

7. Sew three background 2" squares on three corners of the goat 5" x 8" rectangle with a diagonal seam as shown. Sew three dark 2" squares on three corners of a background 3½" x 5" rectangle with a diagonal seam as shown. Trim and press to the dark. Assemble according to the piecing diagram.

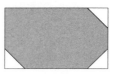

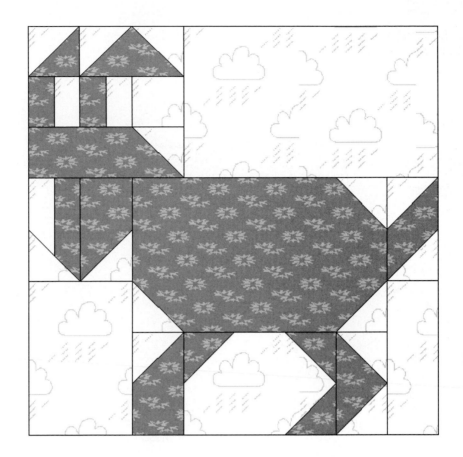

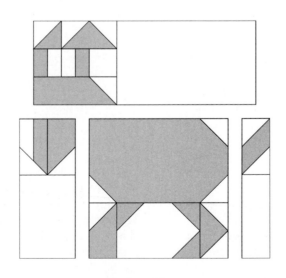

Piecing Diagram

Kangaroo

> 1½" finished square
> 11" x 14" block with seam allowance

Cut for one block:

1.	1 background	5" x 6½"	rectangle
2.	1 background and 1 kangaroo	3⅞"	square
3.	1 background	3½" x 8"	rectangle
4.	2 kangaroo	3½"	square
5.	1 background	2" x 11"	rectangle
6.	3 background and 2 kangaroo	2" x 3½"	rectangle
7.	1 background and 1 kangaroo	1¼" x 22"	strip
8.	4 background and 6 kangaroo	2"	square

Directions:

1. Sew the 1¼" background and kangaroo strips together lengthwise. Press to the dark. Cut five 3½" sections from this strip set for the kangaroo arms, leg, and tail. Then cut one 2" section for a kangaroo ear.

2. Place a kangaroo 2" square on one end of a 3½" strip section and sew a diagonal seam as shown. Outside the stitching, trim fabric to a ¼" seam. Press to the dark. Make 2 of these. Make 1 with a background square. Take one of those with a kangaroo square and place a 2" kangaroo square on the other end. Sew the same diagonal, trim and press.

3. Place a background 2" square on one end of a 3½" strip section and sew a diagonal seam as shown. Trim and press.

4. Place a kangaroo 2" square on one end of a 3½" strip section and sew a diagonal seam as shown. Trim and press. Place a 2" background square on the other end. Sew the same diagonal, trim and press. Make two of these.

5. (A) Place a kangaroo square on a background 2" x 3½" rectangle. (B) Place a background square on a kangaroo rectangle. Sew diagonally to produce the two units as shown. Trim and press.

6. (C) Cut the two 3⅞" squares in half diagonally. Sew together for the kangaroo back. (You will have triangles left for another block.) (D) Place background and kangaroo 2" squares right sides together and sew a diagonal seam. Trim one side to a ¼" seam and press to the dark. This is a 2" half-square. Assemble according to the piecing diagram.

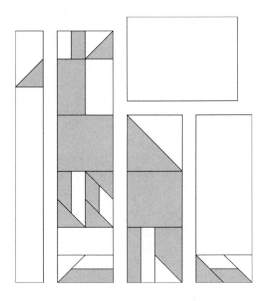

Piecing Diagram

SNAKE

| | 1½" finished square
6½" x 30½" block with seam allowances | | |

Cut for one block:

1.	1 background	3½" x 6½"	rectangle
2.	3 background	3½" x 5"	rectangle
3.	2 background	3½"	square
4.	1 medium and 1 dark	3"	square
5.	2 background	2" x 6½"	rectangle
6.	1 background and 1 medium	2" x 3½"	rectangle
7.	14 background, 30 medium, and 18 dark	2"	square

Directions:

1. Place a background and medium 2" square right sides together and sew a diagonal seam. Trim on one side of the stitching to a ¼" seam allowance. Press to the dark. Make 12 of these. Make another six using dark and medium 2" squares. This is a 2" half-square.

Make 12   Make 6

2. (A) Sew a dark 2" square and a background-medium half-square together as shown. Make 4 of these. (B) Make three reverse. Set two of (A) and one of (B) aside. Add another background-medium half-square to the other four to get two of strip (C) and two of strip (D).

A.   B.

C.   D.

3. Place a medium 2" square on one corner of a 3½" background square. Sew diagonally. Trim outside the stitching to a ¼" seam. Press to the medium. Place a medium 2" square over another corner. Trim and press. Add a dark square and a dark-medium half-square as shown. Make 2 of these.

4. Add a strip (D) on the top, and a strip (C) on the bottom of each of #3. Finally seam a 2" x 6½" strip of background fabric on the right side to make the two wide repeat sections of the Snake block.

Make 2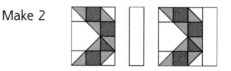

5. Using diagonal seams as above, sew two medium 2" squares on a short side of a 3½" x 5" background rectangle as shown. Trim and press. Add a dark square and a dark-medium half-square as shown. Make 3 of these. These are the narrow repeat sections of the Snake block.

Make 3

6. Make these pieces:
(E) Place one medium 2½" square on the upper right corner of a background 3½" x 6½" rectangle. Sew diagonally, trim, and press.

E.

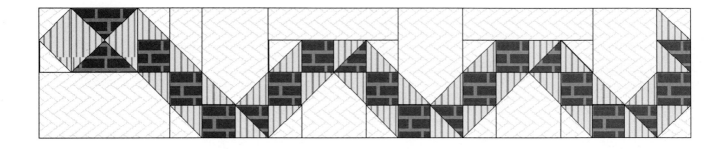

(F) Place a background 2" square on one end of the medium 2" x 3½" rectangle. Sew a diagonal seam as shown. Trim and press. Then place another background square on the other end. Sew the opposite diagonal, trim and press.

F.

(G) Cut the 3" medium and dark squares in half diagonally. Sew together as shown for snake's head. Trim to a 3½" square if necessary. Then sew (E), (F), (G), and one of (A) together as shown to make the head section of the Snake block.

G.

7. Place a medium 2" square on a corner of the background 2" x 3½" rectangle. Sew diagonally, trim and press. Sew this piece to the other (A) (neck strip). Assemble the tail strip from remaining squares and half-squares.

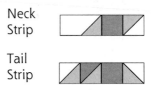

Neck
Strip

Tail
Strip

8. Sew the head, the neck, the narrow repeat sections, the wide repeat sections, and the tail strip together as in the piecing diagram to assemble the Snake block.

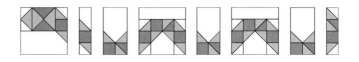

Piecing Diagram

BIRD ON THE GROUND

> 1½" finished square
> 12½" block with seam allowance

Cut for one block:

1.	1 background*	5" x 12½"	rectangle
2.	1 background and 1 bird	3⅞"	square
3.	1 background and 1 bird	3½" x 5"	rectangle
4.	1 background	2" x 6½"	rectangle
5.	2 background and 1 bird	2" x 5"	rectangle
6.	1 background and 1 bird	2" x 3½"	rectangle
7.	8 background and 12 bird	2"	square
8.	1 background and 1 bird	1¼" x 2"	rectangle

*When piecing the Noah's Ark Quilt, make this top strip 3½" x 12½".

Directions:

1. Place a background 2" square on one end of a bird 2" x 3½" rectangle and sew a diagonal seam as shown. Outside the stitching, trim fabric to a ¼" seam. Press to the dark. Place a bird 2" square on one end of a background 2" x 3½" rectangle and sew a diagonal seam as shown (reversed values). Trim and press to the dark.

2. (A) Place a bird 2" square on one end of a background 2" x 5" rectangle and sew a diagonal seam as shown. Trim and press. Make two of these. (B) Take one of these and place a bird square on the other end. Sew the opposite diagonal, trim and press. (C) Place a background 2" square on one end of a bird 2" x 5" rectangle and sew a diagonal seam as shown. Trim and press to the dark. (D) Place a bird 2" square on one end of a background 2" x 6½" rectangle and sew a diagonal seam as shown.

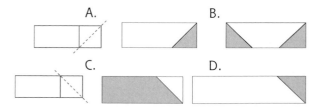

3. Sew two bird 2" squares to two corners of a 3½" x 5" background rectangle with diagonal seams as shown. Trim and press.

4. Cut the background and bird 3⅞" squares in half diagonally. Sew one of each of the resulting triangles together to make a large half-square. (You will have one of each left for another block.)

5. Place a background and a bird 2" square right sides together and sew a diagonal seam. Trim on one side of the stitching to a ¼" seam allowance. Press to the dark. Make five of these. This is a 2" half-square. Assemble according to the piecing diagram.

BIRD ON THE GROUND

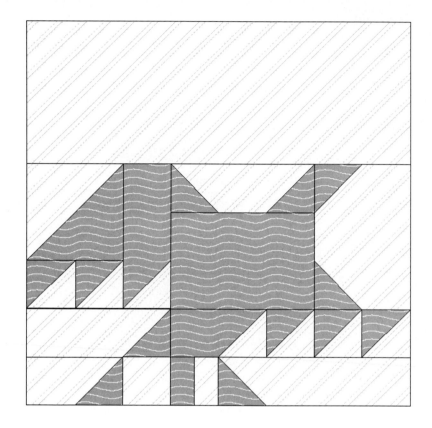

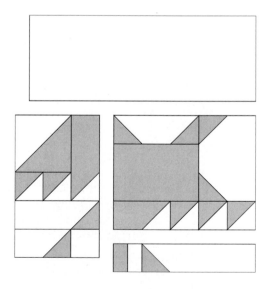

Piecing Diagram

BIRD FLYING

1½" finished square
12½" block with seam allowance

Cut for one block:

1.	1 background	5" x 8"	rectangle
2.	1 bird	5"	square
3.	2 background and 2 bird	3⅞"	square
4.	1 background	3½" x 5"	rectangle
5.	3 background and 1 bird	2" x 5"	rectangle
6.	1 background and 2 bird	2" x 3½"	rectangle
7.	6 background and 8 bird	2"	square

Directions:

1. Place the background and bird 3⅞" squares right sides together. Draw a corner to corner diagonal line on the back of the lightest fabric. Sew ¼" away on both sides of the drawn line. Cut on the line to produce two large half-squares. Make three of these. (You will have one left over for another block.) Place a background 2" square on the bird corner of one of these 3½" half-squares. Sew diagonally, trim, and press to the bird fabric.

2. (A) Place a bird 2" square on one end of a background 2" x 5" rectangle and sew a diagonal seam as shown. Outside the stitching, trim fabric to a ¼" seam. Press to the rectangle. Make three of these. (B) Take one of (A) and place a bird square on the other end. Sew the opposite diagonal, trim and press. (C) Sew a background 2" square on a bird 2" x 5" rectangle with a diagonal seam as shown.

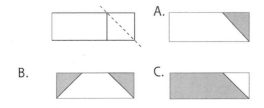

3. Place a background 2" x 3½" rectangle on the right end of a bird 2" x 3½" rectangle and perpendicular to each other. Sew a diagonal seam as shown. Trim and press to the dark.

4. Place a background and bird 2" square right sides together and sew a diagonal seam. Trim on one side of the stitching to a ¼" seam. Press to the dark. Make three of these. This is a 2" half-square.

5. Sew a bird 2" square on one corner of the 3½" x 5" background rectangle with a diagonal seam as shown. Trim and press to the rectangle. Assemble according to the piecing diagram.

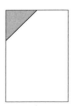

BIRD FLYING

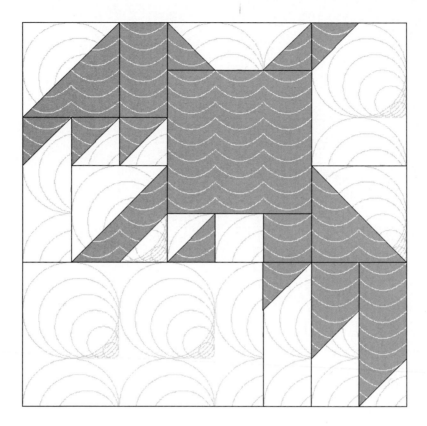

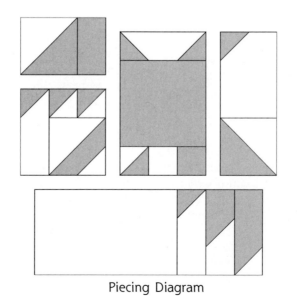

Piecing Diagram

BIRD CIRCLING

1½" finished square
12½" block with seam allowance

Cut for one block:

1.	1 background	5" x 9½"	rectangle
2.	2 background and 2 bird	3⅞"	square
3.	1 background	3½"	square
4.	2 bird	2" x 5"	rectangle
5.	1 background	2" x 8"	rectangle
6.	3 background and 6 bird	2" x 3½"	rectangle
7.	12 background and 10 bird	2"	square

Directions:

1. Place the background and bird 3⅞" squares right sides together. Draw a corner to corner diagonal line on the back of the lightest fabric. Sew ¼" away on both sides of the drawn line. Cut on the line to produce two large half-squares. Make three of these. (You will have one left over for another block.) Place a background 2" square on the bird corner of one of these 3½" half-squares. Sew diagonally, trim, and press to the bird fabric. Make two of these.

2. Place a background 2" square on one end of a 2" x 3½" bird rectangle. Sew a diagonal as shown. Outside the stitching line, trim the fabric to a ¼" seam allowance. Press to the rectangle. Make three of these. Make one with the seam sewn to the opposite diagonal.

Make 3   Make 1

3. Place a bird square on one end of a background 2" x 3½" rectangle. Sew a diagonal seam as shown. Trim and press. Make two of these. Take one of these and place a 2" bird square on the other end. Sew the opposite diagonal.

Make 2

4. Place a background 2" square on one end of a 2" x 5" bird rectangle. Sew a diagonal seam as shown. Trim and press.

5. Place a background and bird 2" square right sides together and sew diagonally. Trim one side to a ¼" seam allowance. Press to the dark. Make three of these. This is a 2" half-square. Assemble according to the piecing diagram.

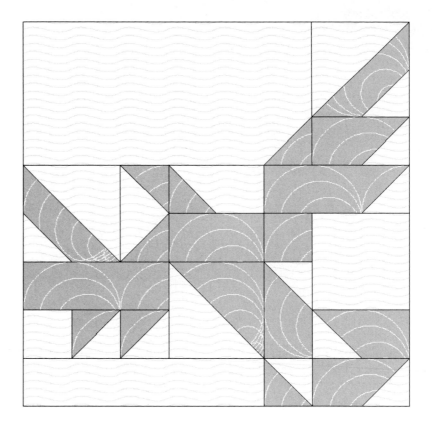

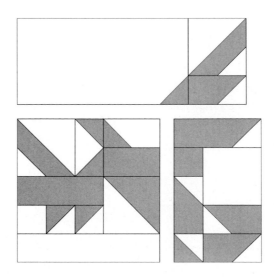

Piecing Diagram

CAMEL

1½" finished square
12½" x 14" block with seam allowance

Cut for one block:

1.	1 background	5" x 6½"	rectangle
2.	1 camel	3½" x 6½"	rectangle
3.	1 background	3½"	square
4.	1 background	2" x 11"	rectangle
5.	1 background	2" x 6½"	rectangle
6.	1 background and 1 camel	2" x 5"	rectangle
7.	1 background and 3 camel	2" x 3½"	rectangle
8.	1 background and 1 camel	1¼"	strip
9.	9 background and 12 camel	2"	square

Directions:

1. Sew the background and camel 1¼" strips together lengthwise. Press to the dark. Then cut the following sections from this set of strips:

1.	3	6½" section
2.	1	5" section
3.	1	3½" section
4.	1	2" section

2. Make these pieces:
(A) Place a background 2" square on one end of a camel 2" x 3½" rectangle and sew a diagonal seam as shown. Outside the stitching, trim fabric to a ¼" seam. Press to the dark.

(B) Place a camel 2" square on one end of a background 2" x 5" rectangle and sew a diagonal seam as shown. Trim and press to the dark.

(C) Place a background 2" square on one end of a camel 2" x 5" rectangle and sew a diagonal seam as shown. Trim and press to the dark. Place another background 2" square on the other end and sew the opposite diagonal seam. Trim and press to the dark.

(D) Place a background 2" square on one end of a camel 2" x 3½" rectangle and sew a diagonal seam as shown. Place another background 2" square at the other end. Sew the same diagonal. Trim and press to the dark.

3. Use the strip sections to make these pieces:
(E) Place a camel 2" square on one end of a 5" strip section as shown and sew a diagonal seam according to the diagram. Trim and press to the triangle.

(F) Place a camel 2" square on one end of a 6½" strip section as shown and sew a diagonal seam according to the diagram. Trim and press to the triangle. Place another 2" square on the other end of this strip section and sew the opposite diagonal seam. Trim and press. Make three of these.

F.

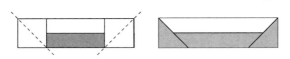

(G) Place a camel 2" square on one end of a 3½" strip section as shown and sew a diagonal seam according to the diagram. Place another camel 2" square at the other end. Sew the same diagonal. Trim and press to the triangles.

G.

(H) Place a 2" strip section and a background 2" square right sides together and sew a diagonal seam according to the diagram. Trim on one side of the stitching as shown to a ¼" seam allowance. Press to the triangle. Assemble according to the piecing diagram.

H.

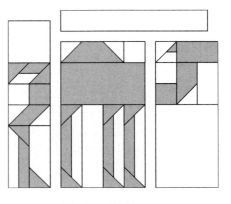

Piecing Diagram

PALM TREE

1½" finished square
12½" x 15½" block with seam allowance

Cut for one block:

1.	1 background	5" x 6½"	rectangle
2.	2 background	3½" x 5"	rectangle
3.	2 palm and 2 background	3⅞"	square
4.	1 palm	3½"	square
5.	1 background	2" x 6½"	rectangle
6.	3 background and 1 palm	2" x 5"	rectangle
7.	4 background and 6 palm	2" x 3½"	rectangle
8.	12 background and 13 palm	2"	square

Reverse Palm Tree Block

Directions:

1. Place a background and palm 2" square right sides together and sew a diagonal seam. Trim on one side of the stitching to a ¼" seam allowance. Press to the dark. Make four of these. This is a half-square.

2. Cut two background and two palm 3⅞" squares in half diagonally. Then sew one of each of the resulting triangles together as shown to make a large half-square. Make three of these.

3. Make these pieces:
(A) Place a background 2" square on one end of a palm 2" x 3½" rectangle and sew a diagonal seam as shown. Outside the stitching, trim fabric to a ¼" seam. Press to the dark. Make four of these.

A.

(B) Place a background 2" square on the other end of (A) and sew the opposite diagonal seam. Trim and press. Make two of these.

B.

(C) Place a palm 2" square on one end of a background 2" x 3½" rectangle and sew a diagonal seam as shown. Trim and press. Make two of these.

C.

(D) Place a palm 2" square on the other end of (C) and sew the same diagonal. Trim and press.

D.

(E) Place a palm 2" square on one end of a background 2" x 5" rectangle and sew the diagonal seam as shown. Make another with the opposite diagonal. Trim and press.

E.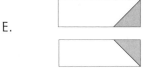

(F) Place a palm 2" square on one end of a background 2" x 6½" rectangle and sew the diagonal seam as shown. Trim and press.

F.

PALM TREE

(G) Place a background 2" x 3½" rectangle on one end of and perpendicular to a palm 2" x 3½" rectangle as shown. Sew a diagonal seam according to the diagram. Trim and press. Make two of these.

3. Sew two palm 2" squares on two corners of the background 3½" x 5" rectangle with diagonal seams as shown. Trim and press. Sew a palm 2" square on one corner of the background 5" x 6½" rectangle with a diagonal seam as shown. Trim, press. Assemble according to the piecing diagram.

G.

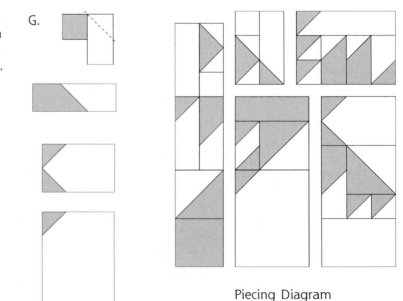

Piecing Diagram

HORSE

	1½" finished square 12½" block with seam allowance

Cut for one block:

1.	1 horse	5" x 6½"	rectangle
2.	1 background and 1 horse	3⅞"	square
3.	2 background	3½" x 6½"	rectangle
4.	1 background	2" x 5"	rectangle
5.	3 background and 1 horse	2" x 3½"	rectangle
6.	4 background and 6 horse	2"	square
7.	1 background and 1 horse	1¼"	strip
8.	1 background	1¼" x 2"	rectangle

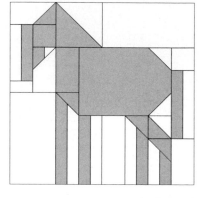

Reverse Horse Block

Directions: *(Note: Make all the pieces in #2, #3, and #4 below in reverse to make a reverse horse block!)*
1. Sew the background and horse 1¼" strips together lengthwise. Press to the dark. Then cut these sections from this set of strips:

1.	1	6½" section
2.	3	5" section
3.	1	3½" section
4.	1	4¼" section
5.	1	2" section

Reverse Head

2. Sew the 1¼" x 2" background rectangle to the 4¼" strip section as shown (head).

3. (A) Place a horse 2" square on the right end of the 6½" strip section (horse strip on the top) and sew a diagonal seam as shown. Outside the stitching, trim fabric to a ¼" seam. Press to the square.

A.

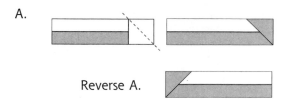

Reverse A.

(B) Place a horse 2" square on the right end of one 5" strip section according to the diagram (horse strip on the top). Sew a diagonal seam as shown. (C) Do the same with the 3½" strip section. Trim and press to the square.

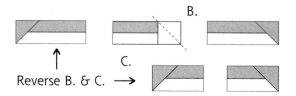

B.

C.

Reverse B. & C. →

(D) Place a horse 2" square on one end of a background 2" x 3½" rectangle and sew a diagonal seam as shown. Trim and press to the square.

D.

Reverse D.

(E) Place the 2" strip section on a 2" x 3½" background rectangle according to the diagram. Sew a diagonal seam as shown, trim and press to the rectangle.

E.

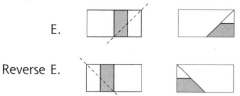

Reverse E.

4. Cut the background and horse 3⅞" square in half diagonally. Sew one of each of the resulting triangles together as shown (neck). *(You will have one of each left for another block.)*

5. Sew two background 2" squares on one short end of the horse 5" x 6½" rectangle with diagonal seams as shown. Trim and press to the rectangle.

6. Place a background and horse 2" square right sides together and sew a diagonal seam. Trim excess fabric on one side of the stitching to leave a ¼" seam. Press to the dark. This is a half-square. Assemble according to the piecing diagram.

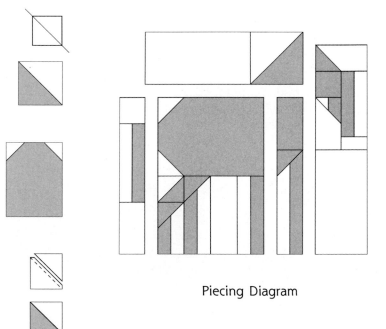

Piecing Diagram

MONKEY

> 1½" finished square
> 12½" block with seam allowance

Cut for one block:

1.	1 background	5"	square
2.	2 background and 2 monkey	3⅞"	square
3.	2 background	3½" x 5"	rectangle
4.	1 monkey	3½"	square
5.	1 monkey	2" x 5"	rectangle
6.	3 background and 2 monkey	2" x 3½"	rectangle
7.	1 background and 1 monkey	1¼" x 13"	strip
8.	10 background and 8 monkey	2"	square

Directions:

1. Place the background and monkey 3⅞" squares right sides together. Draw a corner to corner diagonal line on the back of the lightest fabric. Sew ¼" away on both sides of the drawn line. Cut on the line to produce two large half-squares. Make three of these. (You will have one left over for another block.) Place a background 2" square on the monkey corner of one of these 3½" half-squares. Sew diagonally, trim, and press to the monkey fabric (base of tail).

2. Sew the background and monkey 1¼" strips together lengthwise. Press to the dark. Then cut the following sections from this set of strips:

1.	3	3½" section
2.	1	2" section

3. (A) Place a monkey 2" square on one end of a background 2" x 3½" rectangle and sew a diagonal seam as shown. Outside the stitching, trim fabric to a ¼" seam. Press to the dark. Make two of these.

A.

(B) Place a background 2" square on one end of a monkey 2" x 3½" rectangle. Sew a diagonal seam as shown. Place another background square on the other end. Sew the same diagonal again.

B.

(C) Place a monkey 2" square on one end of a 3½" strip set according to the diagram. Sew a diagonal seam as shown. Trim and press to the square. Make another one with the diagonal in the opposite direction.

C.

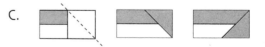

4. Sew a background and a monkey 2" square right sides together with a diagonal seam. Trim away the fabric on one side to a ¼" seam allowance. Press to the dark. Make three of these. This is a 2" half-square.

5. Sew a monkey 2" square on one end of a background 3½" x 5" rectangle with a diagonal seam as shown. Trim and press to the dark. Sew two background 2" squares on two corners of a monkey 3½" square with a diagonal seam as shown. Trim and press to the dark. Assemble according to the piecing diagram.

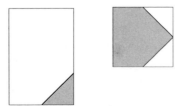

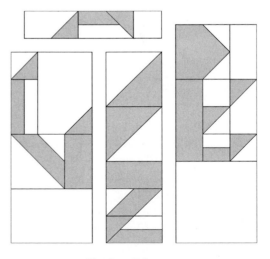

Piecing Diagram

BEAR

| 1½" finished square |
| 14" x 20" block with seam allowance |

Cut for one block:

1.	1 bear	9½" x 12½"	rectangle
2.	1 background and 1 bear	6⅞"	square
3.	1 bear	5" x 6½"	rectangle
4.	1 background	5"	square
5.	1 bear	3½" x 5"	rectangle
6.	1 bear	3½"	square
7.	1 background	2" x 8"	rectangle
8.	1 background	2" x 6½"	rectangle
9.	1 background	2" x 5"	rectangle
10.	3 background and 1 bear	2" x 3½"	rectangle
11.	7 background and 4 bear	2"	square
12.	1 background and 1 bear	1¼" x 2"	rectangle

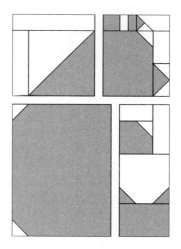

Piecing Diagram

Directions:

1. Place a background 2" square on one end of a bear 2" x 3½" rectangle and sew a diagonal seam as shown. Outside the stitching, trim fabric to a ¼" seam. Press to the dark. Place a 2" background square on the other end. Sew the opposite diagonal, trim and press.

2. Place a background and bear 2" square right sides together and sew a diagonal seam. Trim on one side of the stitching to a ¼" seam allowance. Press to the dark. Then place this half-square right sides together on one end of a background 2" x 3½" rectangle as shown and sew a diagonal seam according to the diagram. Trim and press to the background.

3. Cut the 6⅞" background and bear squares in half diagonally. Take one of each of the resulting triangles and sew together as shown (bear neck). *(You will have one of each left for another block.)*

4. With a diagonal seam:
(A) Sew a background 2" square on one corner of the 3½" bear square.

A.

(B) Sew two bear 2" squares on two corners of the background 5" square as shown.

B.

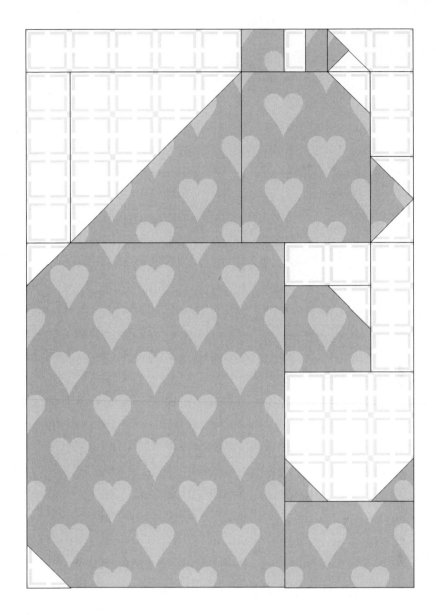

(C) Sew one background 2" square on the upper right corner of the 5" x 6½" bear rectangle.

(D) Sew two background 2" squares to corners on a long side of the 9½" x 12½" bear rectangle. Assemble according to the piecing diagram.

C.

D.

GRIZZLY

1½" finished square
12½" x 18½" block with seam allowance

Cut for one block:

1.	1 grizzly	6½" x 9½"	rectangle
2.	1 background	5"	square
3.	1 grizzly and 1 background	3⅞"	square
4.	1 grizzly	3½" x 11"	rectangle
5.	1 grizzly	3½" x 9½"	rectangle
6.	1 grizzly	3½" x 6½"	rectangle
7.	1 background	3½" x 5"	rectangle
8.	1 background	2" x 5"	rectangle
9.	1 grizzly and 3 background	2" x 3½"	rectangle
10.	1 grizzly and 1 background	1¼" x 8"	strip
11.	7 grizzly and 7 background	2"	square

Directions:

1. Sew the grizzly and background 1¼" strips together lengthwise. Then cut a 2" section and a 5" section from this strip set.

2. Place a 2" background square right sides together on one end of the 5" strip section as shown and sew diagonally according to the diagram. Trim outside the stitching to leave a ¼" seam and press. (Reverse this for the reverse grizzly.)

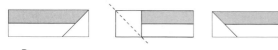

Reverse

3. Place the background and grizzly 3⅞" squares right sides together and draw a corner to corner diagonal line on the back of the light square. Sew ¼" away on both sides of the drawn line. Cut on the drawn line to produce two large half-squares. You will need only one for each Grizzly block.

4. Place a grizzly 2" square right sides together with a background 2" square and sew a diagonal seam as shown. Outside the stitching, trim fabric to a ¼" seam. Press to the dark. This is a 2" half-square.

5. Piece the following units:
(A) Sew a background 2" square diagonally on the upper right corner of the 3½" x 6½" grizzly rectangle with a diagonal seam as shown (upper left for the reverse grizzly).

A.

Reverse

(B) Sew a background 2" square diagonally on the upper right corner of the 6½" x 9½" grizzly rectangle with a diagonal seam as shown (upper left for the reverse grizzly).

B.

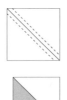

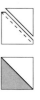

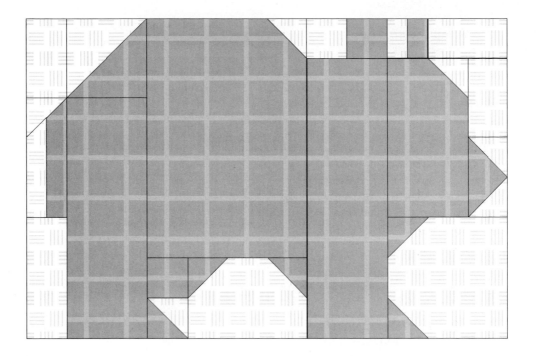

(C) Sew two grizzly 2" squares on two corners of the 5" background square with opposite diagonal seams as shown.

C.

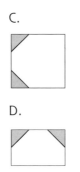

(D) Sew two grizzly 2" squares on two corners of the 3½" x 5" background rectangle with opposite diagonal seams as shown.

D.

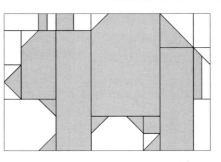

Reverse Grizzly Block

6. Place a background 2" square on one end of a grizzly 2" x 3½" rectangle and sew a diagonal seam as shown. Outside the stitching, trim fabric to a ¼" seam. Press out. Place a background 2" square on the other end. Sew the opposite diagonal, trim and press. Assemble according to the piecing diagram.

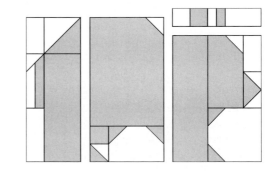

Piecing Diagram

POODLE

1½" each finished square
16½" each finished block

Cut for one block*:

1.	1 poodle	5" x 12½"	rectangle
2.	1 background	5" x 8"	rectangle
3.	1 poodle	5" x 3½"	rectangle
4.	1 background	5" x 3⅛"	rectangle
5.	1 background	5" x 2⅜"	rectangle
6.	2 background and 1 poodle	5" x 2"	rectangle
7.	2 background	3½" x 6½"	rectangle
8.	1 background and 3 poodle	3½"	square
9.	1 background	3½" x 2¾"	rectangle
10.	2 background and 3 poodle	3½" x 2"	rectangle
11.	7 background and 1 poodle	3½" x 1¼"	rectangle
12.	21 background and 7 poodle	2"	square
13.	1 background 1 poodle	2" x 1¼"	rectangle

Face Section

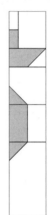

*These pieces are referred to below by their numbers on this cutting chart.
You may wish to pin the pieces together and label them by number.

Directions:

For poodle feet (and tail): Sew a background 1¼" x 3½" (#11 in chart) strip on both sides of three poodle 3½" squares (#8). Press. Then sew a 2" background square diagonally on each corner. Trim outside the stitching to a ¼" seam and press out. Make three altogether.

For the Face Section:
(from the top down)
(A) Sew the poodle and background 2" x 1¼" rectangles (#13) together on the short end. Sew this strip as shown to the left of a 3½" x 2¾" background rectangle (#9).

A.

(B) Place a background 2" square on the right end of a 3½" x 2" poodle rectangle (#10). Sew diagonally as shown. Trim to a ¼" seam and press out.

B.

(C) Place a poodle 2" square on the lower left corner of the background 3½" square. Sew the diagonal. Trim and press.

C.

(D) Sew a poodle and a background 3½" x 2" rectangle (#10) together lengthwise.

D.

(E) Place a poodle 2" square on the upper left corner of a 3½" x 6½" background rectangle (#7). Sew diagonally. Trim and press. Assemble the Face Section according to the diagram.

E.

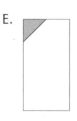

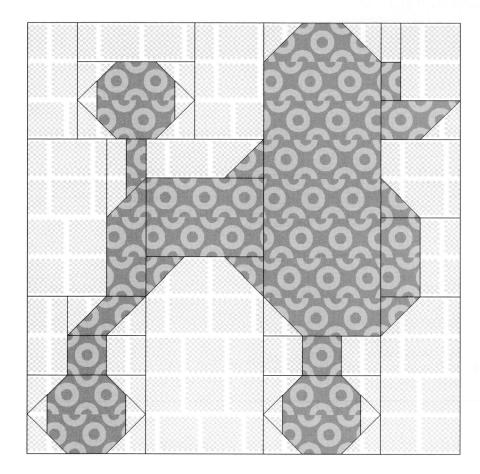

For the Shoulder Section:

(from the top down)

(F) Place a background 2" square at each top corner and the bottom left corner of the poodle 5" x 12½" rectangle (#1). Sew all three diagonals, trim to a ¼" seam and press out.

Shoulder Section

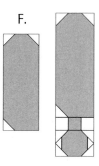

F.

(G) Sew a background 2" square on both sides of a poodle 2" square. Add a poodle foot and assemble according to the diagram.

G.

For the Body Section:

(from the top down)

(H) Place a poodle 2" square on the right side of a background 2" x 5" rectangle (#6). Sew diagonally as shown. Trim and press.

Body Section

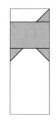

H.

(I) Place two poodle 2" squares at the two top corners of a background 5" x 8" rectangle (#2). Sew diagonally, trim the seam, and press. Add a 5" x 3½" poodle rectangle (#3) between (H) and (I), and assemble according to the diagram.

I.

For the Leg Section:

(from the top down)

(J) Sew the background and poodle 3½" x 1¼" rectangles (#11) together lengthwise. Place a poodle 5" x 2" rectangle (#6) on the right end of this strip set. Sew the diagonal as shown. Trim the seam to ¼" and press out into a unit as shown. Sew this unit on the right side of a background 3½" x 6½" rectangle (#7).

Leg Section

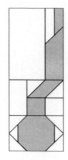

J.

(K) Place a background square on the right end of a 3½" x 2" poodle rectangle (#10). Sew the diagonal as shown. Trim and press. Place a background square on the other end and sew the diagonal in the same direction. Trim and press again. *(Be sure the diagonal is going in the right direction, this unit does have a reverse.)*

K.

(L) Sew a poodle 2" square to a background 2" square. Sew this set to the diagonal unit above. Then sew a background 3½" x 2" rectangle (#10) on the left side of these two units as shown. Add a poodle foot and assemble according to the diagram.

L.

For the Tail Section:

(M) Sew a 5" x 2" background rectangle (#6) on the top of the last poodle foot (for the tail). Then sew the 5" x 3⅛" background rectangle (#4) on the right side and the 5" x 2⅜" background rectangle (#5) on the left side. Assemble all five sections according to the piecing diagram.

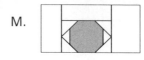

M.

Piecing Diagram

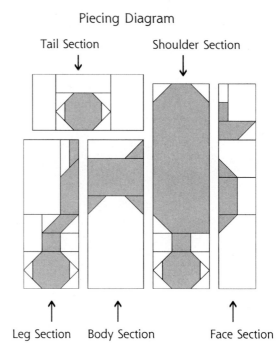

Tail Section   Shoulder Section

Leg Section   Body Section   Face Section

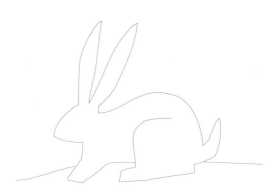

Out To Pasture; 70½" x 76½", features fabrics that shade from one color to another, or from light to dark, across the width of the yardage. Cutting pieces and sewing them back together produces interesting edges and shading effects. Give this as a gift for someone's retirement! Machine quilted by Barbara Ford.

Birds In The Air; 38" x 47", reminds the author of a neighborhood flock of crows. When they are flying and landing, it dazzles the eye like the spots and checkerboards in these fabrics. Machine quilted by Barbara Ford. (below right)

Northwoods; 26" x 32". Nighttime colors, evergreen trees, and a mouse, put the owl in its proper setting. The circular design in the yellow print is centered to add dimension to the owl's eyes. Other careful fabric choices add details to feathers, branches, and the starry sky. Pieced and hand quilted by Betty Parks.

Three Blind Mice; 41" x 39½".
These mice must be blind, since they
don't even see the cat nearby. Make this
quilt as a gift for your favorite feline
to rest on, dreaming. Pieced by Annette
Austin, machine quilted by Lynnette
Baxter, and some hand quilting
by the author.(above)

Panda Bear Quilt; 39½" x 48½".
A simple quilt uses graphic fabric and
high contrast to make a great impression. The bright yellow background
insures a happy mood. Pieced and hand
and machine quilted by Julie Stewart.
(above left)

Little Bird Baby Quilt;
48½" x 48½". The details in these
fabric designs bring out the theme of
feathers and sky. Checkered patterns are
used in both large and small scale.
Combining a group of fabrics from the
same manufacturer/designer adds a
richness and depth to texture and color,
because it all works together. Fabrics
from Concord House.

Penguin Patchwork; 42½" x 51½".
Ice and snow, rocks and water, are the
natural environment of the penguin.
Nature is echoed in this color scheme. The
butler-like formal wear of this bird makes
a strong repeat pattern. Pieced by Annette
Austin, hand quilted by Laura Collier.

Bears 'n Squares; 64½" x 80½".
Black and white with bright colors make an
exciting high-contrast coverlet that any child
would love to own. The large scale of the
design makes a quilt from only four blocks.
Pieced by Lynn Williams and hand quilted
by Laura Collier.

Bunnies and Squirrels Baby Quilt;
51½" x 53". A high-contrast color scheme
of navy, brick red, and white-on-white treats
each animal as a silhouette. The result brings
back memories of illustrations in antique
storybooks or schoolbooks. Pieced by
Annette Austin and hand quilted by
Tammy Mohiswarnath.

Africa; 78½" x 96½". Like TV nature shows of herding animals, this quilt has them lined up in rows. Terri used African fabrics to carry out the theme. This same plan could be used for another ecosystem. Animals of the North, for example. Then wintry fabrics and subdued colors could be used. Pieced by Terri Shinn and hand quilted by Sara Nephew.

Jumping Frogs; 81½" x 90½". This frog block is reminiscent of Native American designs. Because of its balanced simplicity, it could be used as an abstract design in a number of settings. Tammy used these vertical rows to make a rainbow of colored frogs. It is possible that frogs actually come in all these colors. Pieced and machine quilted by Tammy Mohiswarnath.

Noah's Ark Child's Quilt; 54½" x 67½". Heki chose fabrics that bring out something special in each of the animals. Plaid for the Scotty dog, a marvelous textured stripe on the fawn, a feathery print that lets you almost feel the wing of the duck. Even the water under the Ark has a circular design turning it into rolling waves. Her addition to the corner squares makes the whole quilt twinkle. Pieced by Heki Hendrickson.

Small Africa; 50" x 50". Careful fabric choices add realistic details to these animals. Notice the elephant's ear, formed entirely by the dark and light of the fabric print. Eda added beads for eyes. Pieced by Eda Haas and machine quilted by Becky Kraus.

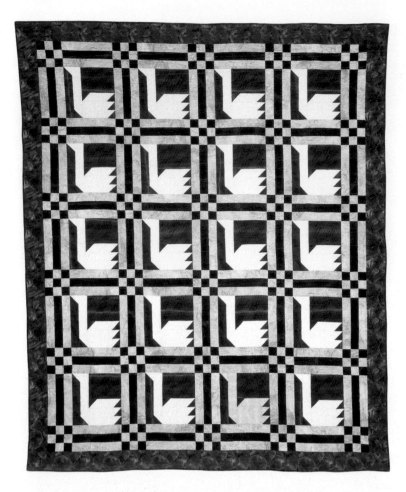

Goose In The Pond; 86½" x 104½". One gray goose swims with all his white companions. The combination of strongly contrasting colors, repetitive blocks, and a geometric setting turns this into a highly effective flowing abstract design. The author chose this traditional nine-patch setting without knowing that it was named "Goose in the Pond". Pieced by Lynn Williams and machine quilted by Laura Peterson.

Butterflies and Flowers; 84½" x 84½". Solids and prints in many clear, light colors were chosen for the wings of the butterflies. A busy floral ties it all together, like a meadow with beautiful wings flickering everywhere in the sunshine. Pieced and machine quilted by Carolann Palmer.

Family Time; 45½" x 47", shows a cat surrounded by playful kittens. Soft colors and pleasant textures make a relaxing picture to contemplate. Pieced and hand quilted by Dee Morrow.

Garden Cats;
85½" x 94½". Resting in the sun and idly contemplating a couple of butterflies, these cats make a pretty picture among the flowers. Will they find some catnip planted there? The large flower print adds to the flickering, sunlit image. Pieced by Shirley Lyons and machine quilted by Susan Lohse.

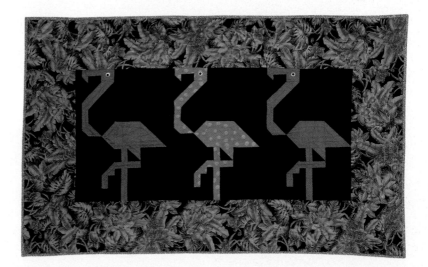

Flamingo Fun; 43" x 26½". A tropical garden surrounds the balancing birds. Eyes were required, so circles were cut out of polka-dot fabric and appliquéd on. Different fabric choices might inspire different eyes. For example; buttons, beads, embroidery, even glue-on eyes like the ones used for fabric toys. Hand quilted.

The Clever Fox;
45½" x 39½". The earthy colors of this simple wall hanging have a masculine feel, and evoke crisp fall air, country living, and apples and cheese for lunch. This could be a sign hanging over the door of an English pub. Machine quilted by Barbara Ford.

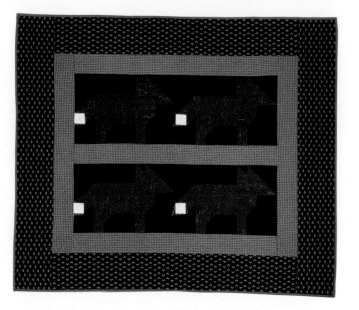

Mustangs; 61" x 74". Sky fabric and two colorways of grass fabric work together to make the perfect background for horse blocks. A slightly lighter background fabric was used around the horses' legs and head to eliminate the visual confusion that would result from the striped sky going in different directions. When these blocks were finished, the author took them along to show her granddaughter. Taylor (then four) took a good look at them on the floor and then picked them up and ran into the bedroom. They had to be given back so the quilt could be finished. Maybe it should be Taylor's quilt? Machine quilted by Barbara Ford.

Deer Crossing: 72½" x 83".
A country look of plaids and checkerboards combines with a country theme of open forest, fields, and a few deer. This simple quilt conveys a restful feeling. Hand quilted by Esther Friesen.

Serpentine: 60½" x 66½".
Virginia decided to do this quilt because her son loves snakes. Doing research, she chose fabrics and colors close to the patterns of the real reptiles. Buttons made eyes, and the name of each snake was embroidered near the tail. Pieced by Virginia Anderson and machine quilted by Lynette Baxter.

Kangaroo Quilt:
52½" x 60½". Cleo chose Australian fabrics to make this richly textured design. Four blocks make a quilt. Could this be a woodland "Roo", moving in and out of shady areas? Pieced by Cleo Nollette and machine quilted by Tammy Stoll.

Ready to Ride;
72½" x 84½". Rich dark colors and a busy floral print produce an appealing quilt. Proud stallions are standing in a field of flowers. Just right for an English country cottage. Pieced by Judy Pollard and machine quilted by Hazel Montague.

Chicken Coop; 53" x 53".
Inspired by the subject matter, Joan searched for just the right fabric to convey straw and feathers. Then her flock seemed to need eyes. An assortment of polka dot fabrics were rejected but this black-on-blue dot seemed to bring out the best in all the other fabrics, adding zing to the quilt. So she titled this quilt "Blue-eyed Chickens". Pieced and hand quilted by Joan Dawson.

74

Eight Reindeer; 60½" x 78½". This quilt was originally going to simply repeat the block in three rows of three, but the author's husband said, "It has to be eight reindeer! " When asked why, his answer was simple. "Dasher, Dancer, Prancer, Vixen...". Later others suggested adding Rudolph. Pieced by Annette Austin and hand quilted by Rose Herrera.

Farmyard; 48½" x 53". Negative-positive blocks, high contrast and strong colors make a bright child's quilt. The horse stands in a ray of sunshine. Machine quilted by Barbara Ford. (below right)

My Window; 30½" x 45½", combines a few blocks for a realistic effect. Light gray-blue sky, feathery bird fabrics, and a textured print that looks like wood helps carry out the theme. Dee added buttons and beads for eyes. Pieced and hand quilted by Dee Morrow. (below)

Ducks in a Row; 85¼" x 92¾". A playful approach to fabric use makes an interesting quilt with lots to look at. Try breaking a few rules once in a while! All fabrics are from Nancy Martin's "Roommates" collection. Pieced by Joan Dawson, Sara Nephew and Terri Shinn. Hand quilted by Sara Nephew.

Pig Pen; 42½" x 42½". A choice of highly textured fabrics and bright color adds a lot of action to this little quilt. Terri thought the pattern name was too plain, and was looking for a great title for her quilt. With these fabric choices, the author suggested "Pork Flambé". Pieced and tied with embroidery stitches (a technique called *chicken tracks*) by Terri Shinn.

Grizzly Bears; 91½" x 100½". An assortment of dark, light and medium fabrics were chosen for bears, trees, and background, and then used almost at random to produce a scrappy look. As blocks were pieced, they were laid out in order to help the author decide which fabrics to use next. Continuous rearrangement resulted in this final layout. Made completely of woven plaids from Mission Valley Textiles. Machine quilted by Barbara Ford.

Animal Sampler; 75½" x 86". A mix of animals and colors is pulled together by a viney print, the same fabric in three different colorways. Some of the larger animals needed eyes, so various sizes of printed black-on-white dots were appliquéd on. The hand quilting is done in concentric rings, **zoo**ming in on each animal.

Moose Country:
70½" x 74½". A simple block shows a moose up to his knees in snow or water. The author tried to include a blue moose, after being told of this Alaskan custom. But somehow the blue block didn't end up in the finished quilt. The black and white trees combine with the snowflake print to produce a chilly image on a warm quilt. Hand quilted by Esther Friesen.

Scotty Dogs: 33½" x 45½". A formal, masculine feel is added to this simple little wall hanging by the fabric choices. Black textured prints imitate dog fur, and the plaids of the Scotty's heritage are placed in the corner blocks. Diane chose to use light fabrics in the center vertical setting strips, thus opening up the design. Pieced by Diane Coombs.

Best in Show: 51½" x 51½". Joan insisted that a poodle be included in the book. Then she assisted with the design process. This eager little fellow is happy to be surrounded by flowers. A bouquet for the winner! Pieced and hand quilted by Joan Dawson.

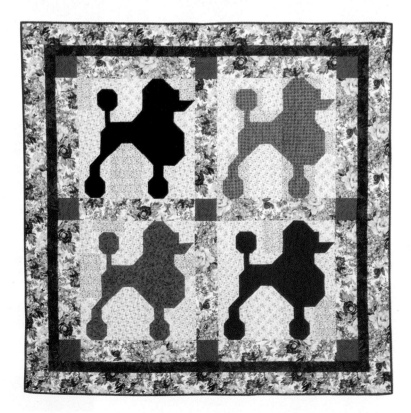

79

Noah's Ark;
82¼" x 94¼".
A childlike approach to fabric choices and so many familiar animals makes this a fun quilt that pleases the eye. The animals can be moved around within their own vertical row to improve the color arrangement. Every place you look, there is something new to see. The borders are quilted in a pattern of waves, carrying out the theme of the Ark. Pieced by Darlene Swenson and machine quilted by Irene Chang.

Oasis; 36½" x 42½". This little quilt could be a Christmas wall hanging (think of it as the background for a crèche), or a reminder of a trip to the Middle East. All together are yellow sand, the desert sky, palm trees, and camels. Hand quilted.

80

INDEX OF QUILTS

37 Patterns

ABOUT EYES

The animal blocks in this book are essentially pieced silhouettes, with distinguishing features that call an individual animal to mind. Careful choice and placement of fabric can add the impression of textures like fur and feathers. In some cases, the quilter may wish to bring out additional details with embellishment. Permanent pen markings, paint, embroidery, appliqué, even beads, buttons, etc., could add ears, mouths, or eyes.

Eyes on these animals may not be necessary most of the time for a number of reasons: 1. Our imagination supplies many details in the identification of the animal. The author has heard students talking about what the animal will eat and what it's doing as they are piecing a block. 2. Many of these blocks are like large animals seen from too great a distance to pick up such small details as eyes. 3. In nature, wild animals avoid eye contact. So the head turns or the animal runs away. 4. Do we want a quilt that has eyes all over it, staring back at us?

Still, to fulfill the potential of a design, eyes are sometimes absolutely necessary. One way of adding eyes that is efficient and in keeping with most fabric choices is to find a fabric with spots or dots on it (usually white fabric with black spots). Cut out a circle or other shape, and appliqué this "eye" to the animal block. At the right you will find actual-sized copies of the eyes the author added to the Animal Sampler quilt. Add approximately ¼" of fabric outside these outlines and appliqué, turning under the seam allowance. (For a bird's eye, see the directions in the Little Bird Baby Quilt, pg. 92.)

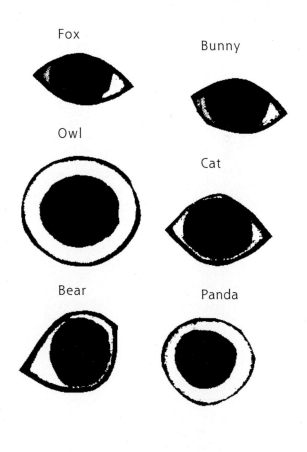

Fox

Bunny

Owl

Cat

Bear

Panda

BEST IN SHOW

1½" finished square
Quilt with borders: 51½" x 51½"

All fabric 44" prewashed
Fabric requirements:
1 yd. poodle fabric
1 yd. background fabric
¾ yd. fabric for setting strips
⅓ yd. inner border fabric
¾ yd. outer border fabric

Directions:
(Blocks should measure 16½" each. If the size varies, adjust the setting strips to the average measurement of the blocks.)
Make four Poodle blocks according to the directions on pg. 62. Cut 12 setting strips 3½" x 17", and nine 3½" corner squares. Sew the blocks in two vertical rows, each row having two blocks separated by a setting strip. Use the remaining setting strips and corner squares to make the vertical strips that join and frame the poodle rows. Add a 2" inner border and a final 3½" outer border.

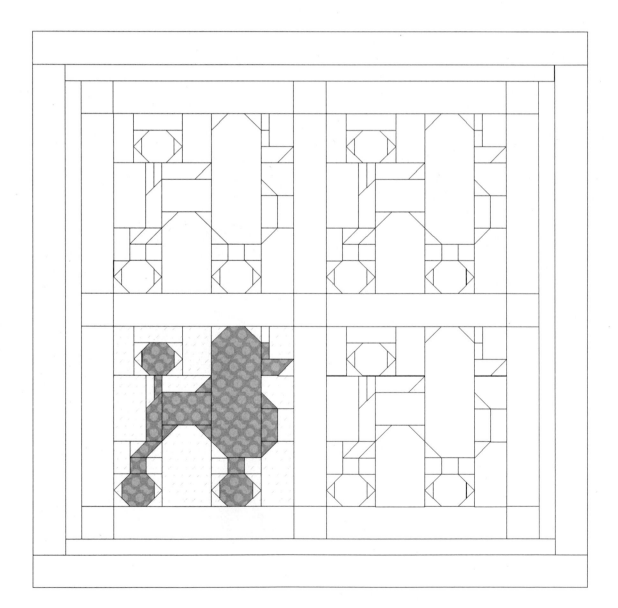

FLAMINGO FUN

All fabric 42" wide prewashed.
Fabric requirements:
¼ yd. flamingo fabric
¼ yd. pink fabric (dotted)
⅔ yd. black fabric
⅓ yd. navy blue fabric
⅔ yd. border fabric (tropical print)

Directions:

Make three Flamingo blocks according to the directions on pg. 36. Sew the blocks together in a horizontal row. Add a final 6½" border.

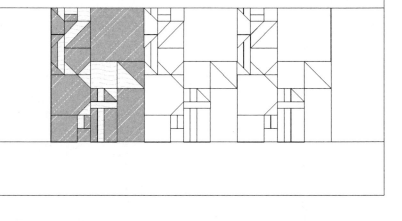

OASIS

All fabric 42" wide prewashed.
Fabric requirements:
½ yd. camel fabric
½ yd. palm tree fabric
⅛ yd. sky fabric
1 yd. background fabric
⅛ yd. fabric for setting strips
½ yd. inner border fabric
¾ yd. outer border fabric

Directions:

1. Make two Camel blocks according to the directions on pg. 50. Add a 3½" x 14" rectangle of sky fabric to the top of each Camel block.

2. Make one Palm Tree block and one reversed Palm Tree block according to the directions on pg. 52. Sew two horizontal rows according to the quilt diagram, with a 2" x 15½" setting strip between two blocks. Sew the rows together as shown with a 3½" x 27½" horizontal setting strip between. Add a final 5½" outer border.

BUTTERFLIES AND FLOWERS

1½" finished square
Quilt with borders: 84½" x 84½"

All fabric 42" wide prewashed.
Fabric requirements:
1⅓ yds. butterfly fabric (solids and pastel prints)
¼ yd. black for body
1¼ yds. background fabric
1½ yds. flower squares
1 yd. inner setting strips
1 yd. outer setting strips
⅓ yd. flower centers
1⅓ yds. border fabric

Directions: 1. Cut for 16 blocks:

1.	2 butterfly	5"	square
2.	2 butterfly	3½"	square
3.	2 background	2" x 11"	rectangle
4.	2 background	2" x 3½"	rectangle
5.	1 background	2"	strip
6.	1 body	6½"	strip
7.	192 background	2"	square

2. Sew the 2" strip of background fabric and the 6½" strip of body fabric together lengthwise. Press to the dark. Cut into 16 sections 2" wide. This is the butterfly body. Then follow the directions (except #3) on pg. 9 and make 16 Butterfly blocks.

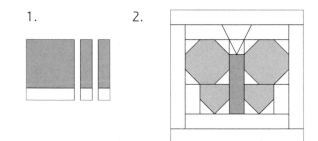

3. Enlarge each Butterfly block by sewing a 2" x 11" background framing rectangle on the left and right and a 2" x 14" background framing rectangle on top and bottom. (Now blocks should measure 14". If the size varies, adjust the setting strips to the average of the block measurement.)

4. Cut for setting:

1.	32 background	2" x 11"	rectangle
2.	32 background	2" x 14"	rectangle
3.	25 flower center	3½"	square
4.	3 inner setting	8"	strip
5.	1 outer setting	14"	strip
6.	4 flower petal	3½"	strip

5. (A) Sew two flower petal 3½" strips lengthwise on both sides of an 8" inner setting strip. Press to the dark. Make three of these. Cut into 3½" sections. You will need 40 sections. (If a few more are needed, cut individual 3½" squares of petal fabric and 3½" x 8" rectangles of inner setting fabric.) This is an inner setting unit. (B) Sew a flower petal 3½" strip lengthwise on one side of a 14" outer setting strip. Press to the dark. Cut into 3½" sections. You will need 16 of these. (If a few more are needed, cut individual 3½" squares of petal fabric and 3½" x 14" rectangles of outer setting fabric.) This is an outer setting unit.

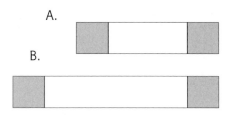

6. Make four vertical rows of Butterfly blocks, alternating blocks and inner setting units, beginning and ending with an inner setting unit. Make five vertical rows of inner setting units, alternating with 3½" square flower centers. Begin and end with a flower center. Sew the block rows and setting rows together alternately as in the quilt diagram. Sew the outer setting units together in four sets of four. Cut four 3½" squares of petal fabric and four squares of outer setting fabric. Add a petal square to one end of each strip where needed. Sew two outer setting strips on the left and right of the quilt top. Add a square of outer setting fabric to each end of the two remaining strips. Sew on the top and bottom. Add a final 5" border.

BUTTERFLIES AND FLOWERS

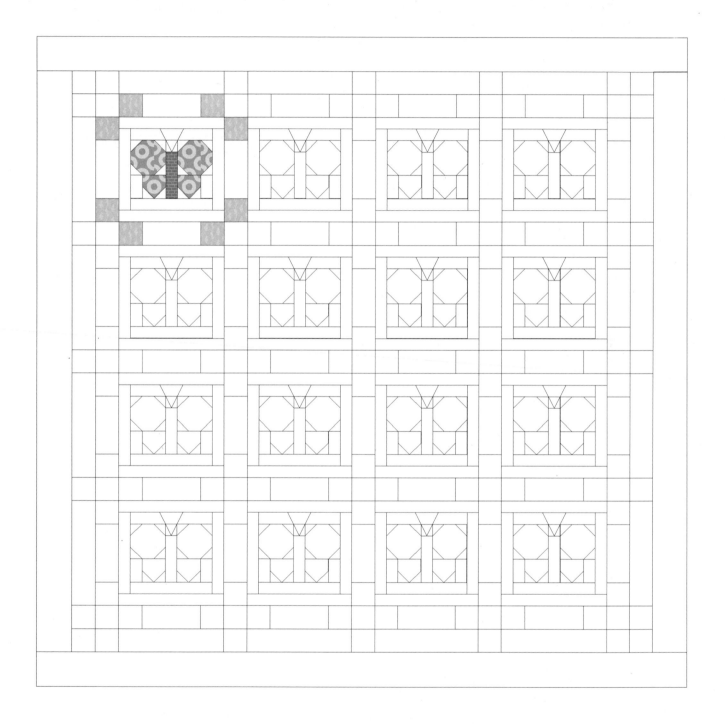

PENGUIN PATCHWORK

All fabric 42" wide prewashed.
Fabric requirements:
⅓ yd. background fabric
¼ yd. penguin fabric
⅛ yd. beak fabric
½ yd. alternate block fabric
¼ yd. yellow setting rectangle
¼ yd. blue setting rectangle
½ yd. inner border
1 yd. outer border

1½" finished square
Quilt with borders: 42½" x 51½"

Directions:

1. Make nine Penguin blocks according to the directions on pg. 2; OR Cut for nine Penguin blocks:

1.	9 background and 18 penguin	2" x 6½"	rectangle
2.	1 background and 1 penguin	1¼" x 19"	strip
3.	72 background, 9 beak, and 27 penguin	2"	square

2. Sew background and penguin 1¼" strips together lengthwise. then cut nine 2" sections from this set of strips.

3. Place a background and beak 2" square right sides together and sew a diagonal seam. Trim on one side of the stitching to a ¼" seam allowance. Press to the dark. This is a half-square. Make nine of these (penguin beak). Make 18 half-squares from penguin and background 2" squares (penguin foot).

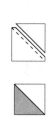

4. Continue to make the blocks according to the directions on pg. 2. Then cut:

1.	9	3½" x 5"	blue setting rectangle
2.	9	3½" x 5"	yellow setting rectangle
3.	9	5" x 9½"	alternate plain block

5. Sew a blue rectangle to the bottom of each Penguin block and a yellow rectangle to the bottom of each alternate block. Sew into three horizontal rows as shown in the quilt diagram and sew the rows together. Add a 3" inner border and a final 5¼" outer border to complete the quilt.

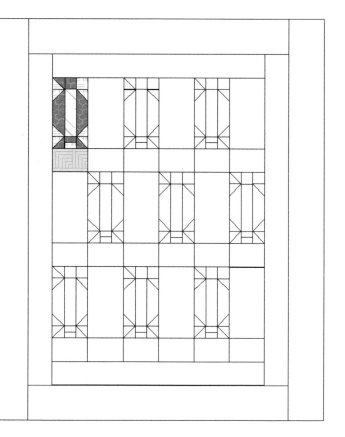

SCOTTY DOGS

1½" finished square
Quilt with borders: 33½" x 45½"

All fabric 42" prewashed.
Fabric requirements:
⅔ yd. dog fabric
1 yd. background fabric
½ yd. fabric for setting strips
⅛ yd. fabric for corner squares
⅓ yd. border fabric

Directions:

1. Cut for six Scotty Dog blocks:

1.	6 dog	5" x 8"	rectangle
2.	6 background	3½" x 5"	rectangle
3.	6 background	2" x 5"	rectangle
4.	6 background, 12 dog	2" x 3½"	rectangle
5.	1 dog	3½"	strip
6.	18 dog	2"	square
7.	1 background	2"	strip

2. Sew the 2" background strip and the 3½" dog strip together lengthwise. (If each Scotty Dog block is made from different fabric, cut 12 dog 3½" x 2" rectangles and 12 background 2" squares.) Cut into 2" sections. Assemble six Scotty Dog blocks according to the directions on pg. 3.

3. Cut for setting strips:
(Block should measure 9½". If the size varies, adjust the setting strip to the average block measurement.)

1.	17 setting fabric	3½" x 9½"	rectangle
2.	12 corner squares	3½"	square

4. Make two vertical rows of Scotty Dog blocks alternating with setting strips, beginning and ending with setting strips. Sew the setting strips and corner squares together to make three setting rows. Sew all rows together alternately. Add a final 3½" border.

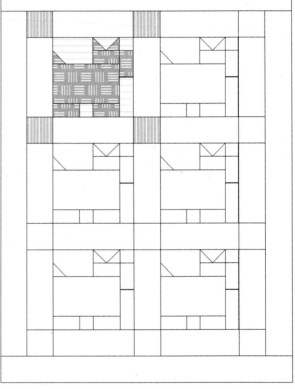

PANDA BEAR QUILT

All fabric 42" wide prewashed.
Fabric requirements:
½ yd. background fabric
¾ yd. black fabric (includes corner squares)
½ yd. white fabric
½ yd. fabric for setting strips
1 yd. border fabric

1½" finished square
Quilt with borders: 39½" x 48½"

Directions:

1. Piece four Panda blocks according to the directions on pg. 7. OR Cut for four Panda blocks:

1.	1 background	5" x 9"	strip
2.	4 white	5" x 6½"	rectangle
3.	8 black	3½" x 6½"	rectangle
4.	1 background and 1 black	2" x 30"	strip
5.	1 white, 1 background, 6 black	2" x 9"	strip
6.	8 background	2" x 6½"	rectangle
7.	16 white	2" x 5"	rectangle
8.	1 white and 1 black	1¼" x 9"	strip
9.	8 white, 24 background, 24 black	2"	square

2. (A) Sew two black and one background 2" x 9" strips together lengthwise as shown. Cut 2" sections from this set of strips for panda inner legs. (B) Sew two black and one white 2" x 9" strips together lengthwise as shown. Cut 2" sections from this set of strips for panda eyes. (C) Sew two black 2" x 9" strips and one background 5" x 9" strip together lengthwise as shown. Cut 2" sections from this set of strips for panda ears. (D) Sew background and black 2" x 30" strips together lengthwise as shown. Cut eight 3½" sections from this set of strips for panda outer legs. (E) Sew the white and black panda 1¼" x 9" strips together lengthwise as shown. Cut 2" sections from this set of strips for panda nose. Continue to piece four Panda blocks according to the directions on pg. 7.

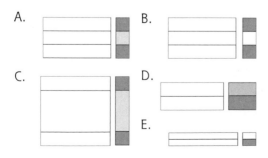

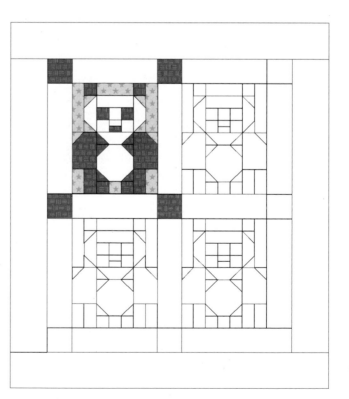

PANDA BEAR QUILT (contd.)

3. Cut:

1.	9	3½"	corner square
2.	6	3½" x 11"	setting strip
3.	6	3½" x 15½"	setting strip

4. Make two rows of two Panda blocks with a 3½" x 15½" setting strip between, beginning and ending with the same setting strip. Make three rows of 3½" x 11" setting strips with a corner square between, beginning and ending with a corner square. Sew together according to the quilt diagram. Add a final 5" border.

BIRD IN THE AIR

1½" finished square
Quilt with borders: 38" x 47"

All fabric 42" wide prewashed.
Fabric requirements:
1 yd. bird fabric
2 yd. assorted sky fabrics
1 yd. outer border fabric

Directions:
1. From the bird and sky fabric piece one of each of these blocks:
Plain Bird pg. 4
Bird on the Ground pg. 44
Bird Flying pg. 46
Bird Circling pg. 48

2. Cut from sky fabrics and sew to blocks as shown:

1.	1	3½" x 12½"	left of Bird Flying
2.	2	12½" x 14"	right of Bird Flying **and**
			top of Bird on the Ground
3.	1	5" x 12½"	right of Bird Circling
4.	1	9½" x 14"	left of Plain Bird
5.	1	6½" x 8"	top of Plain Bird

3. Assemble according to the quilt diagram and add a 5" final border.

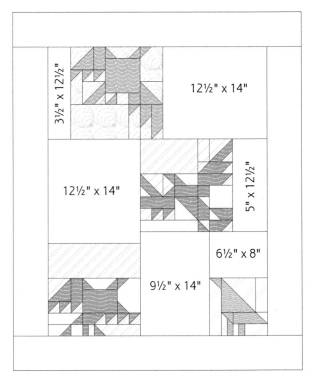

THE CLEVER FOX

1½" finished square
Quilt with borders: 45½" x 39½"

All fabric 42" wide prewashed.
Fabric requirements:
½ yd. fox fabric
½ yd. background fabric
⅔ yd. fabric for setting strips
⅓ yd. white fabric
⅓ yd. black fabric
⅓ yd. border fabric

Directions:
1. Piece four Fox blocks according to the directions on pg. 29.

2. Cut five 3½" x 30½" setting strips. Sew the Fox blocks into two horizontal rows of two and sew the rows together with a setting strip between. Add a setting strip top and bottom. Then add a setting strip left and right. Add a final 6" border to complete the quilt.

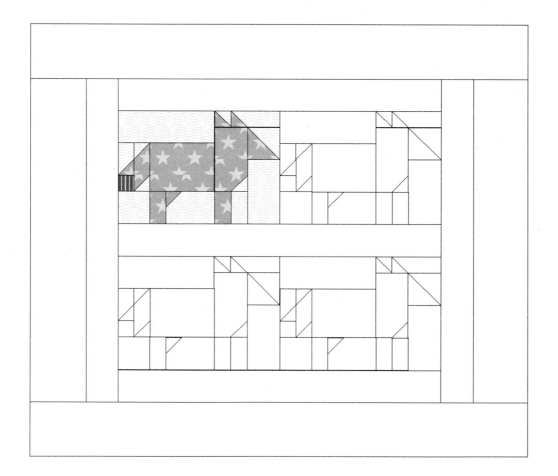

Northwoods

All fabric 42" wide prewashed.

Fabric requirements:
¼ yd. mouse fabric
¼ yd. tree fabric
¼ yd. owl fabric
¼ yd. wing fabric
(if desired, scraps of a different color
for beak, foot and ground under trees)
¼ yd. background fabric
⅓ yd. fabric for setting strips and inner border
⅔ yd. border fabric

Directions:
1. Piece according to the directions on
the following pages:
Owl block pg. 31
Mouse block pg. 4
Christmas Tree block pg. 5 (make two)

2. Cut:

1.	2	2" x 5"	ground fabric
2.	2	2" x 15½"	setting strip

3. Sew the ground fabric on the bottom of
each tree block and sew the two blocks
together vertically. Then with a setting strip
between, sew the tree blocks to the right of
the owl block. Sew the other setting strip to
the top of the Mouse block and sew it to the
bottom of the group, as shown in the quilt
diagram. Add a 2" inner border and a 4¼"
outer border to complete the quilt.

1½" finished square
Quilt with borders: 26" x 32"

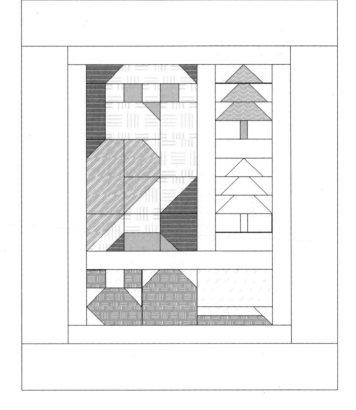

LITTLE BIRD BABY QUILT

1½" each finished square
Quilt with borders: 48½" x 48½"

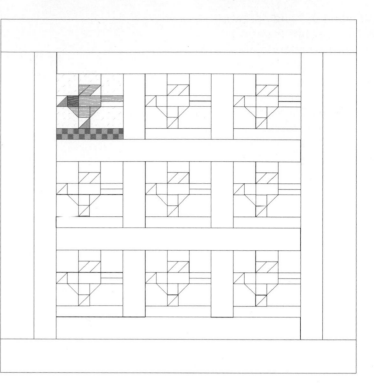

All fabric 42" wide prewashed.
Fabric requirements:
½ yd. bird fabric (¼ yd. each two blues)
2" strip beak fabric
2" strip head fabric
fabric for eyes if desired
1 yd. background fabric
1¼ yd. fabric for setting strips
1¼ yd. fabric for border

Directions:
1. Assemble nine Little Bird blocks,
pg. 24. OR: Cut for nine blocks:

1.	9 background	3½" x 5"	rectangle
2.	27 background	3½"	square
3.	9 background and 18 bird	3½" x 2"	rectangle
4.	9 background and 9 bird	3½" x 1¼"	rectangle
5.	9 bird	2" x 9½"	rectangle
6.	36 background, 36 bird, 18 beak	2"	square

2. Place a background and beak 2" square right sides together and sew a diagonal seam. Trim on one side of the stitching to a ¼" seam allowance. Press to the dark. This is a half-square (bird beak and foot). Make 18 of these.

3. Assemble nine Baby Bird blocks. Add eyes if desired. (I used ¼" black polka dots printed on white fabric. Cut out a larger circle around the dot (about 1") and baste a running stitch ¼" from the cut edge. Draw up the basting stitches and turn the raw edges under with your fingers, manipulating the fabric to make a nice round eye. Use a couple of stitches to hold the raw edges together and in back. Baste to the bird ¼" from the top and front of the head. Then stitch on securely with small invisible stitches.)

4. Cut for setting strips:
(Blocks should measure 9½". If the size varies, adjust the setting strips to the average block size.)

1.	9 rectangles	3½" x 9½"
2.	9 rectangles	3½" x 12½"
3.	1 strip	3½" x 36½"
4.	1 strip	3½" x 39½"

5. Add a 3½" x 9½" setting strip to the right side of each block. Then sew a 3½" x 12½" setting strip to the bottom of each block. Sew the blocks into three rows of three. Sew the rows together. Sew a 3½" x 36½" strip of setting fabric at the top of the quilt and then sew the 3½" x 39½" setting strip at the left side. Add a final 4¾" border to complete the quilt top.

CHICKEN COOP

1½" finished square
Quilt with borders: 53" x 53"

All fabric 42" wide prewashed.
Fabric requirements:
¾ yd. medium chicken fabric
¼ yd. dark chicken fabric
1 yd. background fabric
¼ yd. inner corner square fabric
1 yd. setting strip fabric
¼ yd. outer corner square fabric
1 yd. border fabric

Directions:
1. Make one Rooster block according to the directions on pg. 15. Make two Hen blocks and six Reverse Hen blocks according to the directions on pg. 14.

2. Cut:

1.	16 corner squares	3½"
2.	24 setting strips	3½" x 11"

3. Sew the blocks into three rows as shown, alternating blocks with setting strips, beginning and ending with setting strips. Sew the remaining setting strips into four rows, alternating setting strips with corner squares, beginning and ending with corner squares. Sew all the rows together.

4. Add a final border: cut 5" strips of fabric 41" long (or the measurement of your quilt top). Sew two of these onto opposite sides of the quilt top. Cut four 5" squares for corners. Sew the squares onto both ends of the two remaining border strips. Sew these onto the other two sides of the quilt.

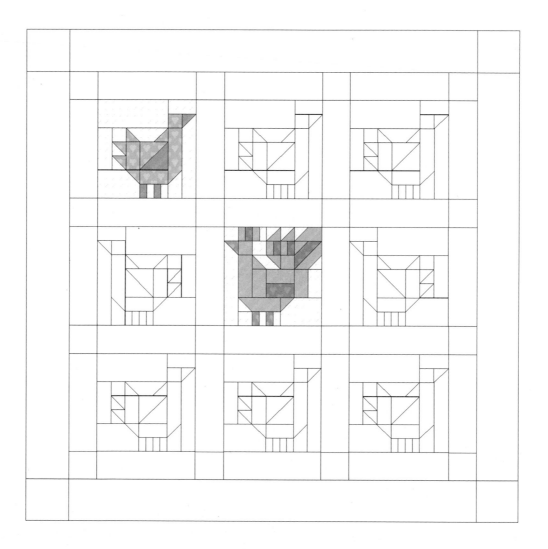

BEARS 'N SQUARES

All fabric 42" wide prewashed.
Fabric requirements:
2 yds. bear fabric
1 yd. background fabric
1⅓ yds. setting strip fabric
¼ yd. corner square fabric
1 yd. each of three different
fabrics for border squares
(or 2 yds. border fabric)

| | | 2" finished square
Quilt with borders: 64½" x 80½" | |

Directions: 1. Cut for four Bear blocks:

1.	4 bear	12½" x 16½"	rectangle
2.	4 background and 4 bear	8⅞"	square
3.	4 bear	6½" x 8½"	rectangle
4.	4 background	6½"	square
5.	4 bear	4½" x 6½"	rectangle
6.	4 bear	4½"	square
7.	4 background	2½" x 10½"	rectangle
8.	4 background	2½" x 8½"	rectangle
9.	4 background	2½" x 6½"	rectangle
10.	12 background and 4 bear	2½" x 4½"	rectangle
11.	28 background and 16 bear	2½"	square
12.	1 background and 1 bear	1½" x 11"	strip

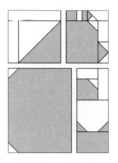

Piecing Diagram

2. Place a background 2½" square on one end of a bear 2½" x 4½" rectangle and sew a diagonal seam as shown. Outside the stitching, trim fabric to a ¼" seam. Press to the dark. Place a 2½" background square on the other end. Sew the opposite diagonal, trim and press.

3. Place a background and bear 2½" square right sides together and sew a diagonal seam. Trim on one side of the stitching to a ¼" seam allowance. Press to the dark. Then place this half-square right sides together on one end of a background 2½" x 4½" rectangle and sew a diagonal seam according to the diagram. Trim and press to the background.

4. Cut the 8⅞" background and bear squares in half diagonally. Take one of each of the resulting triangles and sew together as shown. (bear neck) *(You will have one of each left for another block.)*

A.

5. With a diagonal seam:
A. Sew a background 2½" square on one corner of the 4½" bear square (arm).

B.

B. Sew two bear 2½" squares on two corners of the background 6½" square as shown (foot).

BEARS 'N SQUARES

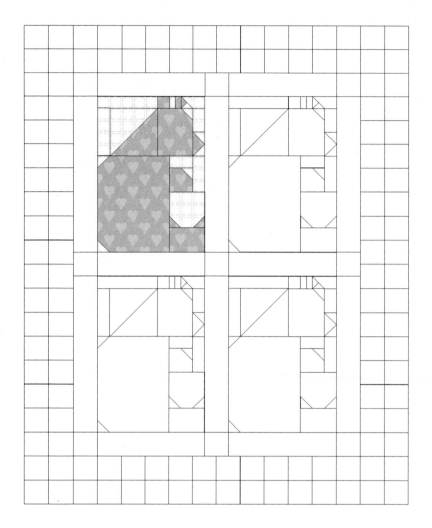

C. Sew one background 2½" square on the upper right corner of the 6½" x 8½" bear rectangle (head).

C.

D. Sew two background 2½" squares to corners on a long side of the 12½" x 16½" bear rectangle (body).

D.

6. Sew the background and bear 1½" strips together lengthwise. Press to the dark. Cut four 2½" sections from this set of strips. Assemble according to the piecing diagram.

7. Cut:

1.	6	4½" x 18½"	setting strip
2.	6	4½" x 26½"	setting strip
3.	9	4½" x 4½"	corner square

8. Sew the bears into two vertical rows with a 4½" x 18½" setting strip between, beginning and ending with the same setting strip. Sew the 4½" x 26½" setting strips into three vertical rows of two, with a corner square between, beginning and ending with a corner square. Sew the rows together according to the quilt diagram.

9. For the border: Cut 128 4½" squares including at least three different fabrics. Make four borders two squares wide and 16 squares long. Sew two borders left and right and then the remaining two borders top and bottom.

DUCKS IN A ROW

1½" finished square
Quilt with border: 85¼" x 92¾"

All fabric 42" wide prewashed.

Fabric requirements:

1 yd. dark duck fabric
¾ yd. medium duck fabric
1¼ yd. background fabric
1¾ yd. fabric for alternate squares
1⅓ yd. fabric for setting strips
½ yd. inner border fabric
2¾ yd. outer border fabric

Directions:

Piece 15 Duck blocks according to the directions on pg. 30. Cut 15 alternate fabric 11" squares. Sew five rows of blocks. Each row has three Duck blocks and three alternate fabric squares. Sew the rows together, with four 5" setting strips between. Add a 1¾" inner border, and a final 10" border to complete the quilt.

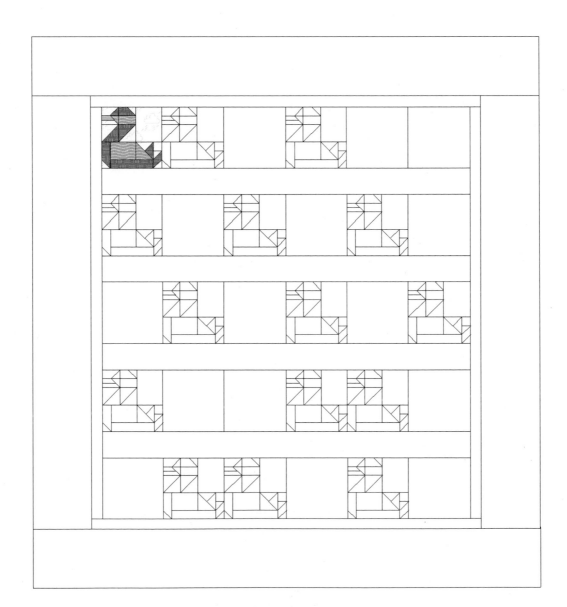

BUNNIES AND SQUIRRELS BABY QUILT

> 1½" finished square
> Quilt with borders: 51½" x 53"

All fabric 42" wide prewashed.

Fabric requirements:
1⅓ yds. bunny/squirrel fabric
1 yd. setting strip fabric
2½ yds. background fabric
1 yd. border fabric

Directions:

1. Make five Bunny blocks according to the directions on pg. 32 and four Big Squirrel blocks according to the directions on pg. 17.

2. Cut:

1.	24 setting strips	3½" x 11"
2.	16 corner squares	3½" x 3½"

3. Sew the animals into rows with setting strips between. The center row has two squirrels and one bunny. The outside rows have two bunnies and one squirrel. Make four rows of setting strips, alternating setting strips and corner squares, beginning and ending with a corner square. Sew all the rows together according to the quilt diagram. Add a final 5" border.

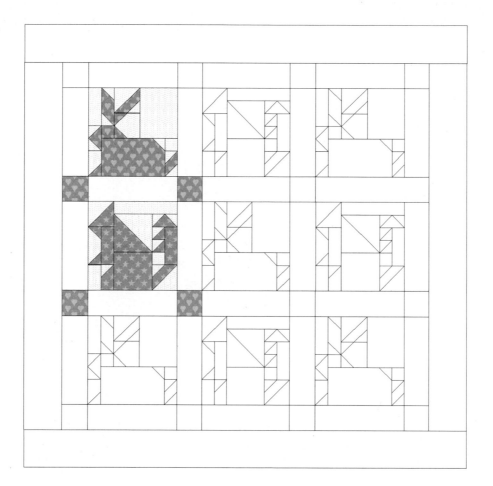

FAMILY TIME

1½" finished square
Quilt with borders: 45½" x 47"

Directions:

1. Make three Kitten blocks and three Reverse Kitten blocks according to the directions on pg. 13. Make one Cat block as on pg. 12.

2. Cut:

1.	6	2" x 9½"	setting strip
2.	2	3½" x 12½"	setting strip
3.	4	6½" x 9½"	fill-in rectangle
4.	2	3½" x 9½"	fill-in rectangle
5.	1	2" x 11"	fill-in strip

3. Add a 2" x 11" strip of fill-in fabric to the bottom of the Cat block. Add a 3½" x 9½" rectangle of fill-in fabric to the top of one Kitten block and one reverse Kitten block. (Use these three blocks for the center horizontal row.)

All fabric 42" wide prewashed.

Fabric requirements:

¼ yd. cat fabric
½ yd. dark kitten fabric
½ yd. other kitten fabric
¾ yd. background fabric
⅓ yd. fabric for fill-in pieces
½ yd. setting fabric
¾ yd. border fabric

4. Make a top and bottom horizontal row as shown, using for each row; a Kitten block, a reverse Kitten block, three 2" x 9½" setting strips, and two 6½" x 9½" fill-in rectangles. Sew the three rows together with a 2" setting strip between, according to the quilt diagram. Add a 2" border of setting fabric and a final 5" border.

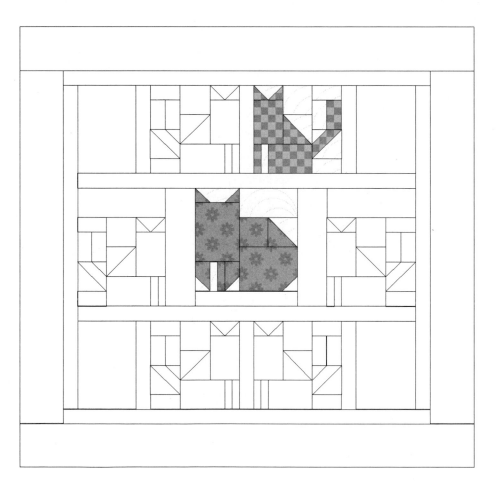

THREE BLIND MICE

1½" finished square
Quilt with borders: 41" x 39½"

Directions:

1. Cut for one double-sized Kitten block:

1.	1 background and 1 kitten	6⅞"	square
2.	2 kitten	6½" x 9½"	rectangle
3.	1 background	6½"	square
4.	5 background and 2 kitten	3½" x 6½"	rectangle
5.	2 background and 3 kitten	3½"	square
6.	1 background and 1 kitten	2" x 6½"	rectangle

All fabric 42" wide prewashed.
Fabric requirements:
¼ yd. kitten fabric
¼ yd. mouse fabric
1½ yd. background fabric
½ yd. border fabric

2. Cut one background and one kitten 6⅞" square diagonally. Sew one background and one kitten of the resulting triangles together (kitten back). You will have one of each left for another block.

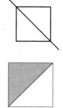

3. Sew the background and kitten 2" x 6½" rectangles together lengthwise (kitten leg).

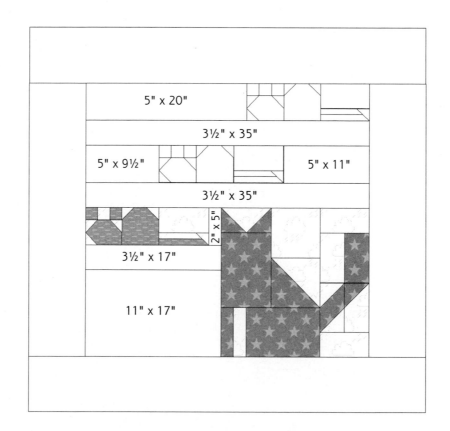

3. (A) Place a kitten 3½" square on one end of a background 3½" x 6½" rectangle. Sew diagonally as shown. Trim outside the stitching to a ¼" seam allowance. Make two of these. (B) Place a 3½" kitten square on the other end of one of these units. Sew the opposite diagonal. Trim and press (kitten ears).

A.

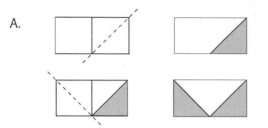

4. Place a background 3½" square on one end of a kitten 3½" x 6½" rectangle. Sew a diagonal as shown, trim and press. Place a second 3½" background square on the other end. Sew the same diagonal line. Trim and press (kitten tail). Assemble according to block diagram.

B.

5. Make three Mouse blocks according to the directions on pg. 4. Then cut:

1.	2 setting	3½" x 35"	strip
2.	1 setting	3½" x 17"	strip
3.	1 fill-in	5" x 20"	rectangle
4.	1 fill-in	5" x 11"	rectangle
5.	1 fill-in	5" x 9½"	rectangle
6.	1 fill-in	2" x 5"	rectangle
7.	1 fill-in	11" x 17"	rectangle

6. Sew the 5" x 20" rectangle of fill-in fabric to the left of the mouse in the top row. Sew a 5" x 9½" rectangle of fill-in fabric to the left, and a 5" x 11" rectangle of fill-in fabric to the right of the mouse in the middle row. Add a 3½" x 35" strip of setting fabric on the bottom of both of these rows.

7. Sew a 2" x 5" rectangle of fill-in (or background) fabric to the right of the bottom mouse. Add a 3½" x 17" strip of setting fabric to the bottom of this mouse. Then sew a 11" x 17" rectangle of fill-in fabric below this short row. Add the Kitten block on the right. Sew all three rows together. Complete the quilt with a final 7½" border.

100

SERPENTINE

Directions:

1. Piece 10 Snake blocks according to the directions on pg. 42. (You may make different colored snakes.)

2. Cut from setting fabric:
(Blocks should measure 6½" x 30½". If this varies, adjust the length of the strips to the average of the blocks.)

1.	5	3½" x 30½"	strip
2.	2	5" x 30½"	strip
3.	4	6½" x 9½"	rectangle
4.	2	6½" x 42½"	strip

3. Sew four Snake blocks with 3½" x 30½" strips between them. Alternate the snakes up and down. Sew the 5" x 30½" strips to left and right of the snakes.

All fabric 42" preshrunk.
Fabric requirements:
2½ yds. background (¼ yd. for one snake)
2½ yds. medium (¼ yd. for one snake)
2½ yds. dark (¼ yd. for one snake)
1¾ yds. setting fabric
1 yd. outer border

4. Sew a 3½" x 30½" strip to the right of two Snake blocks. Sew a 6½" x 9½" rectangle top and bottom. Add one of these sets to the top and to the bottom of the four snakes as shown. Finish top and bottom with a 6½" x 42½" strip. Sew the remaining four Snake blocks into two vertical sets of two. Then sew these to the left and right sides of the quilt top. Add a final 4½" border.

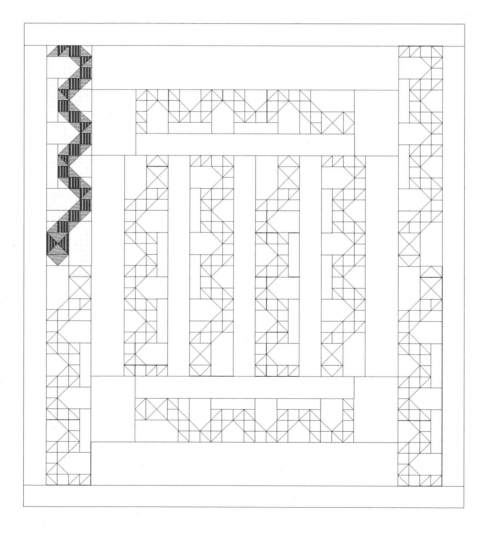

GARDEN CATS

> 1½" finished square
> Quilt with borders: 85½" x 94½"

All fabric 42" wide prewashed.
Fabric requirements:
2 yds. cat fabric
1½ yd. cat background fabric
(scraps of fabric for butterfly wings and body)
2 yds. large floral print for alternate squares
1 yd. setting strips
¼ yd. corner squares
3 yds. border fabric

Directions:
1. Piece 18 Cat blocks according to the directions on pg. 12. OR: Cut for 18 Cat blocks:

1.	36 cat	5" x 6½"	rectangle
2.	9 background and 9 cat	3⅞"	square
3.	18 background	3½" x 6½"	rectangle
4.	18 cat	3½"	square
5.	18 background	2" x 5"	rectangle
6.	36 cat	2" x 3½"	rectangle
7.	2 background and 2 cat	1¼"	strip
8.	54 background 36 cat	2"	square

2. Sew a 1¼" background and cat strip together lengthwise. Press to the dark. Make another one of these. Then cut 18 sections 3½" wide for the cat's paws.

3. Continue to piece according to the directions on pg. 12. Make 18 blocks. Make two Butterfly blocks according to the directions on pg. 9.

4. Cut ten 11" squares of large floral fabric. OR: Cut flowers, etc., out of large floral prints and piece together to make 11" blocks.

5. Cut 36 corner 2" squares. Cut 71 setting strips 2" x 11". Make two vertical rows of Cat blocks, alternating and beginning and ending with setting strips. Make 3 vertical rows of floral blocks. (Insert the Butterfly blocks where you wish.) Begin and end the rows with a Cat block and a setting strip.

6. Make six vertical rows of setting strips and corner squares (seven strips and seven squares to each row). Sew the setting strip rows and block rows together alternately, beginning and ending with a setting strip row. Add a final 11" border.

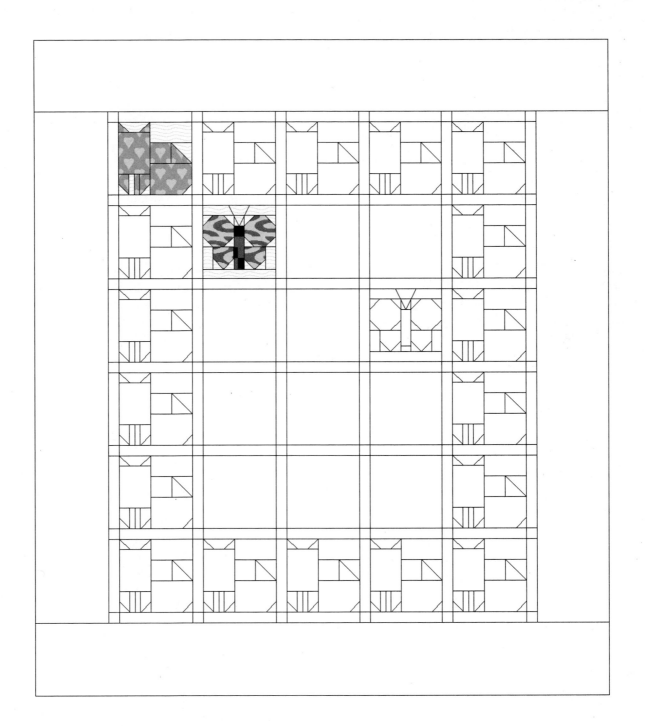

GOOSE IN THE POND

All fabric 42" wide prewashed.
Fabric requirements:
2 yds. goose fabric
2 yds. background fabric
2 yds. dark setting strip fabric
3 yds. background setting strip fabric
1½ yds. border fabric

2" finished square
Quilt with borders: 86½" x 104½"

9-Patch Block

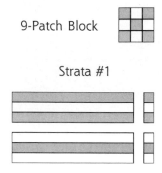

Strata #1

Strata #2

Directions: 1. Cut for 20 Goose blocks:

1.	20 background	6½" x 8½"	rectangle
2.	20 goose	4½" x 6½"	rectangle
3.	20 background and 20 goose	2½" x 12½"	rectangle
4.	20 goose	2½" x 8½"	rectangle
5.	100 background and 60 goose	2½"	square

2. Place a goose 2½" square on one end of a background 2½" x 12½" rectangle and sew a diagonal seam as shown. Outside the stitching, trim fabric to a ¼" seam. Press to the dark. 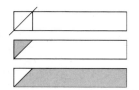 Make 20 of these. Make another twenty of these with reversed values (goose rectangle and background square).

2. Place a background 2½" square on one end of a goose 2½" x 8½" rectangle and sew a diagonal seam as shown. Trim fabric to a ¼" seam. Press to the dark. Place a background 2½" square on the other end. Sew the same diagonal, trim and press. Make 20.

3. Place a background and goose 2" square right sides together and sew a diagonal seam. Trim on one side of the stitching to a ¼" seam allowance. Press to the dark. This is a 2" half-square. Make 40 of these. Assemble 20 Goose blocks according to the piecing diagram.

4. Cut:

1.	25 dark setting fabric	2½"	strip
2.	38 background setting fabric	2½"	strip

5. Sew two dark and one background setting fabric strips into a set of strips as shown. (Strata #1) Press to the dark. Make four of these sets. Sew two background and one dark setting fabric strips into a set of strips as shown. (Strata #2) Press to the dark. Make 17 of these.

6. From Strata #2, cut 12½" sections for Setting Strips. You will need 49 altogether. From the leftover pieces of Strata #2 cut 2½" sections for the 9-Patch blocks. You will need 30 of these. From Strata #1 cut 2½" sections. You will need 60 of these. Use all the 2½" sections to make 30 9-Patch blocks.

7. Make four vertical rows of five Goose blocks each, alternating with horizontal Setting Strips and beginning and ending with Setting Strips. Make five vertical rows of 9-Patches alternating with vertical Setting Strips, beginning and ending with 9-Patch blocks. Sew the rows together according to the quilt diagram. Add a final 4½" border.

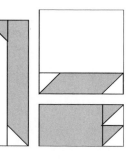

Piecing Diagram

GOOSE IN THE POND

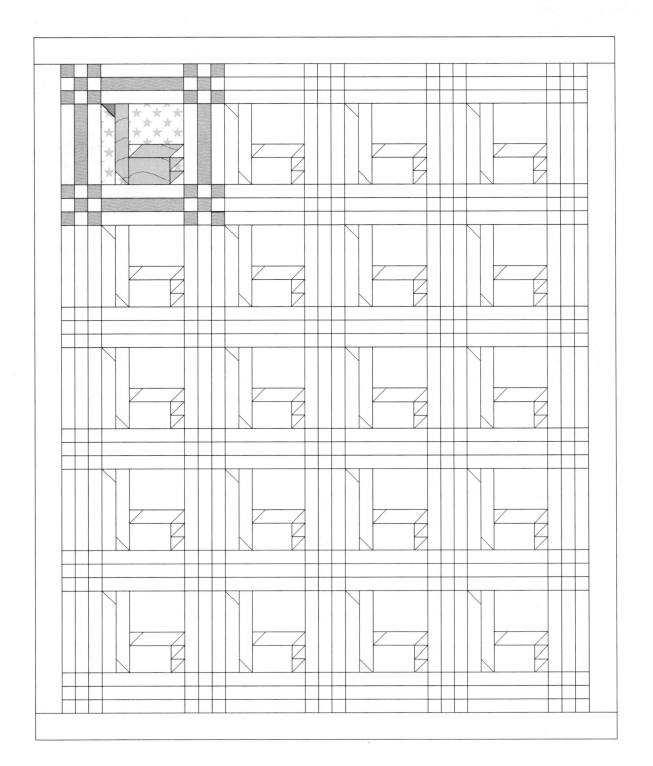

MOOSE COUNTRY

All fabric 42" prewashed.
Fabric Requirements:
1 yd. moose fabric (if using four different fabrics, buy ⅓ yd. each)
1 yd. tree fabric
⅛ yd. trunk fabric
2 yds. background fabric (if using four different fabrics, buy ½ yd. each)
½ yd. setting strips
1 yd. inner border
2 yds. final border fabric

2" finished square
Quilt with borders: 70½" x 74½"

Directions:
1. Cut for four Moose blocks:

1.	4 moose fabric	8½" x 10½"	rectangle
2.	4 background and 4 moose	4½" x 6½"	rectangle
3.	20 background and 16 moose	4½" x 2½"	rectangle
4.	4 background and 4 moose	2½" x 12"	strip
5.	44 background and 32 moose	2½"	square

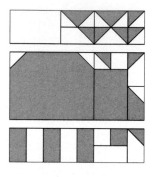

Piecing Diagram

2. Sew the background and moose 2½" strips together lengthwise. This strip set will be 4½" wide. Then cut four 2½" lengths and eight 4½" lengths from this strip.

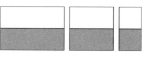

3. Place a moose 2½" square at one end of a background 2½" x 4½" rectangle and sew a diagonal as shown. (A) Trim outside the stitching to a ¼" seam and press. Make 12 of these. (B) Make four with the diagonal in the other direction and set aside. (C) Make 12 with values reversed as shown. (D) Place a background 2½" square on the other end of (C). Sew the opposite diagonal. Trim and press. Make eight of these. (E) Place a moose 2½" square on the other end of (A) and sew the opposite diagonal as shown. Make four of these.

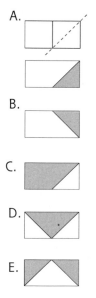

4. Place a background and moose 2½" square right sides together and sew a diagonal seam. Trim on one side of the stitching to a ¼" seam allowance. Press to the dark. Make 12 of these.

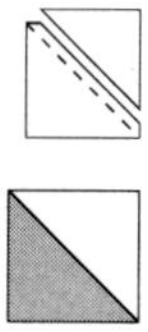

5. Place a background 2½" square on one corner of the moose 8½" x 10½" rectangle. Sew the diagonal, trim, and press. Place a background 2½" square on the other end of the long side, sew, trim, and press. Assemble according to the piecing diagram.

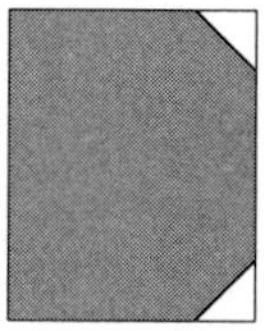

6. Cut for 26 Christmas Tree blocks:

1.	26 tree fabric	2½" x 6½"	rectangle
2.	26 tree fabric	2½" x 5½"	rectangle
3.	26 tree fabric	2½" x 4½"	rectangle
4.	52 background	2½" x 3½"	rectangle
5.	4 background	3"	strip
6.	52 background	2½" x 3"	rectangle
7.	52 background	2½"	square
8.	2 trunk	1½"	strip

7. Sew the 3" background strips on either side of the trunk strip lengthwise. This strip set will measure 6½". Then cut 26 sections 2½" wide for trunks.

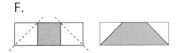

8. (F) Place a background 2½" square on the right end of the tree fabric 2½" x 6½" (#8) rectangle. Sew diagonally as shown. Place another background 2½" square on the other end. Sew the opposite diagonal.

F.

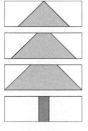

(G) Place a background 2½" x 3" (#3) perpendicular to the right end of a tree fabric 2½" x 5½" (#7) rectangle as shown. Sew the diagonal seam, trim and press. Then do the same on the other side, sewing the opposite diagonal.

G.

(H) Place a background 2½" x 3½" (#5) rectangle perpendicular to the right end of a tree 2½" x 4½" (#6) rectangle. Sew the diagonal seam, trim, and press. Do the same on the left side, sewing the opposite diagonal. Sew four rows together in order.

H.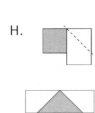

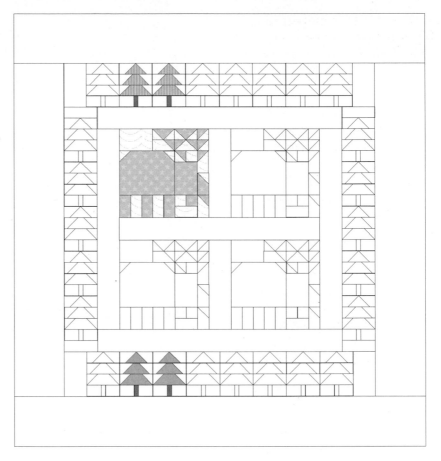

Piecing Diagram

To complete the quilt top:

9. Cut for setting strips and borders: (Blocks should measure 16½". If the size varies, adjust the setting strips to the average of the actual measurements.)

1.	4 background	2½" x 6½"	rectangles
2.	4 background	4½" x 8½"	rectangles
3.	2 inner setting	4½" x 16½"	strip
4.	1 inner setting	4½" x 36½"	strip

10. Sew the Moose blocks into two rows of two blocks each, with a 4½" x 16½" strip of inner setting fabric between. Then sew the rows together with a 4½" x 36½" strip of inner setting fabric between the rows. Add a 4½" inner border. Assemble the Christmas Tree blocks into two horizontal rows of eight trees each, beginning and ending with a 4½" x 8½" rectangle of background fabric. Use the remaining trees to make two vertical rows, beginning and ending with a 2½" x 6½" rectangle of background fabric. Sew the vertical rows onto the Moose blocks first, then the horizontal rows. Add a 7½" outer border to complete the quilt.

EIGHT REINDEER

All fabric 42" wide prewashed.
Fabric requirements:
1 yd. reindeer fabric
1¼ yd. background fabric
⅛ yd. brown fabric
⅛ yd. tree fabric
½ yd. setting strips
½ yd. inner border squares
1 yd. inner border rectangles
1¼ yd. outer border

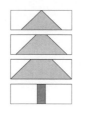

2" finished square
Quilt with borders: 60½" x 78½"

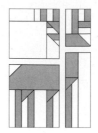

Piecing Diagrams

Directions: 1. Cut for eight Reindeer blocks:

1.	8 background	6½"	square
2.	8 deer	4½" x 8½"	rectangle
3.	8 background	2½" x 12½"	rectangle
4.	8 background	2½" x 6½"	rectangle
5.	16 background and 16 deer	2½" x 4½"	rectangle
6.	9 background and 9 deer	1½"	strip
7.	16 background and 32 deer	2½"	square

D.

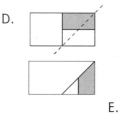

E.

2. Sew the background and deer 1½" strips together lengthwise. Press to the dark. Then cut the following sections from this set of strips for one reindeer:

1.	3	6½"	for eight 24	section
2.	1	8½"	for eight 8	section
3.	1	4½"	for eight 8	section
4.	6	2½"	for eight 48	section

4. (D) Place a 2½" strip section on one end of a background 2½" x 4½" rectangle as shown and sew a diagonal seam according to the diagram. (E) Sew a deer square right sides together with a 2½" strip section as shown.

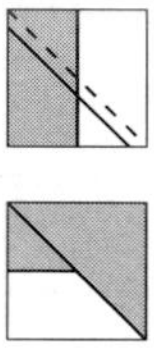

5. Place a background 2½" square on one end of a deer 2½" x 4½" rectangle and sew a diagonal seam as shown. Press to the dark (head). Sew a background 2½" square on one corner of the 4½" x 8½" deer rectangle using a diagonal seam as shown. Trim and press. Assemble according to the piecing diagram.

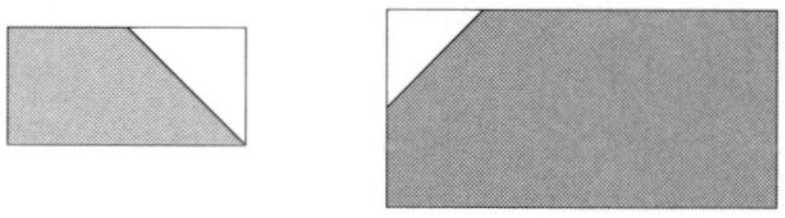

3. Finish the strip sections as follows:
(A) Place a deer 2½" square on one end of a 6½" strip section as shown. Sew a diagonal seam according to the diagram. Trim and press to the dark. (B) Place a deer 2½" square on the other end of a 6½" strip section as shown. Sew the same diagonal. (C) Sew a deer 2½" square on one end of the 8½" strip section as shown.

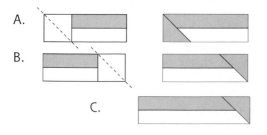

6. Cut for one Christmas Tree block:

1.	1 tree fabric	4½" x 12½"	rectangle
2.	1 tree fabric	4½" x 10½"	rectangle
3.	1 tree fabric	4½" x 8½"	rectangle
4.	2 background	4½" x 6½"	rectangle
5.	4 background	4½" x 5½"	rectangle
6.	2 background	4½"	square
7.	1 brown	2½" x 4½"	rectangle
8.	1 brown	2½" x 12½"	rectangle

7. Place one 4½" x 6½" background rectangle on the right end of and perpendicular to the 4½" x 8½" tree rectangle. Sew a diagonal seam as shown. Trim outside the stitching to a ¼" seam allowance. Press to the background fabric. Place another 4½" x 6½" background rectangle on the other end and sew the opposite diagonal seam. Trim and press to the background fabric.

8. Place one 4½" x 5½" background rectangle on the right end of and perpendicular to the 4½" x 10½" tree rectangle. Sew a diagonal seam as shown. Trim and press to the dark. Place a 4½" x 5½" background rectangle on the other end and sew the opposite diagonal.

9. Place one 4½" background square on the 4½" x 12½" tree rectangle. Sew a diagonal seam as shown. Trim and press to the dark. Place another 4½" background square on the other end. Sew the opposite diagonal seam. Trim and press. Assemble as in the piecing diagram.

10. Cut: *(Note: You may wish to measure your blocks and adjust the length of the setting strips to match.)*

1.	2	2½" x 40½"	setting strip
2.	6	2½" x 18½"	setting strip
3.	12	6½"	red square
4.	4	6½" x 16½"	green rectangle
5.	2	6½" x 14½"	green rectangle
6.	4	6½" x 10½"	green rectangle
7.	2	6½" x 8½"	green rectangle

11. Make three horizontal rows of blocks as shown in the quilt diagram, sewing 2½" strips of setting fabric between the blocks and between the rows. Make two side borders of red squares and green rectangles. Begin with 16½" rectangles at the top and bottom of the side borders, and the 14½" rectangles at the centers. Sew onto the quilt top. Make two top and bottom borders from red squares and green rectangles. The 10½" rectangles are left and right, and the 8½" rectangles are the centers. Begin and end with squares. Sew onto the quilt top. Add a final 4½" border to complete the quilt.

JUMPING FROGS

1½" finished square
Quilt with borders: 81½" x 90½"

All fabric 42" wide prewashed.
Fabric requirements:
2¾ yds. frog color (or five 20" pieces)
1¾ yds. background color
¼ yd. eye color
1¼ yds. setting fabric
2½ yds. border fabric

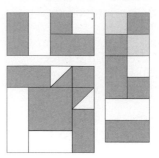

Piecing Diagram

Directions: 1. Cut for 40 Frog blocks:

1.	4 frog	3½"	strip
2.	16 background and 12 frog	2"	strip
3.	40 background	2" x 5"	rectangle
4.	60 frog	2" x 3½"	rectangle
5.	120 frog and 80 background	2"	square
6.	5 eye and 5 frog	2" x 25"	strip

2. Place a background and frog 2" square right sides together and sew a diagonal seam. Trim on one side of the stitching to a ¼" seam allowance. Press to the dark. This is a half-square. Make 80 of these. (Or make 1½" half-squares according to your favorite method.)

3. Sew one background and one frog 2" strip together lengthwise. Press to the dark. Make 12 of these. From this set of strips, cut two 3½" sections (80 altogether) and two 2" sections (80 altogether) for each frog (hands and feet). Sew a dark 2" x 3½" rectangle at the bottom of all the 2" sections, making 20 left and 20 right.

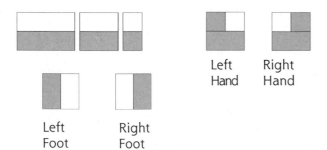

Left Hand

Right Hand

Left Foot

Right Foot

4. Sew one frog and one eye 2" strip together lengthwise. Press to the dark. Make 5 of these. Then cut this strip set into 2" sections (80 are needed). Sew two 2" sections together to make the head.

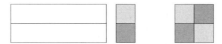

5. Sew one background 2" strip and a frog 3½" strip together lengthwise. Cut a 3½" section from this strip set. Sew a 2" x 5" background strip on the left side of this section (body).

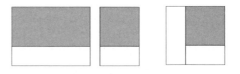

6. Assemble 40 Frog blocks according to the piecing diagram. Sew the Frog blocks into five rows of eight blocks each. The frogs should point to the upper right. Sew the rows together, with a 5" setting strip between. Add a final 9½" border.

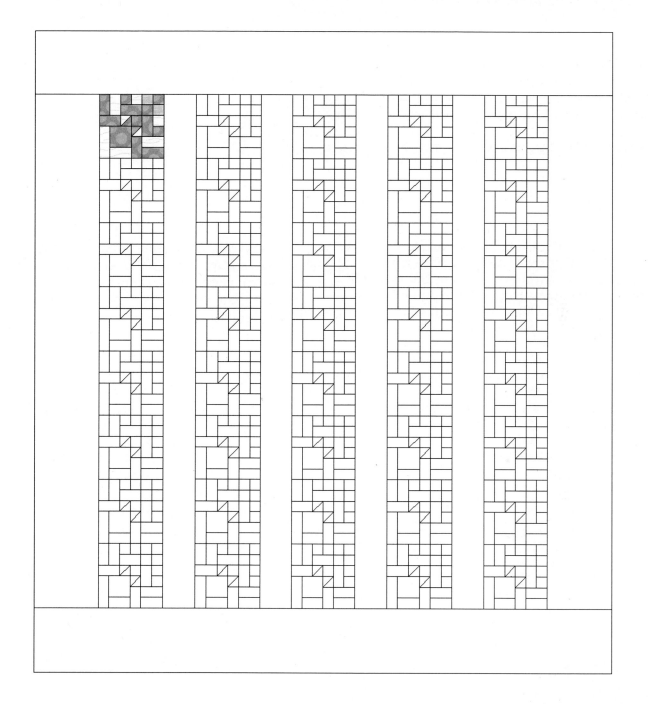

MY WINDOW

1½" finished square
Quilt with borders: 30½" x 45½"

All fabric 42" wide prewashed.
Fabric requirements:
¼ yd. for each animal (Little Bird ⅛ yd.)
¼ yd. each animal background (Little Bird ⅛ yd.)
¼ yd. railing fabric
½ yd. mixed backgrounds between railings
¼ yd. each light, medium, and dark window frame
¼ yd. final border fabric

Directions:
1. Piece a Bird Circling block according to the directions on pg. 48. Piece a Little Bird block and a reverse according to the directions on pg. 24., **but leave off the bottom strip.** Piece a Little Squirrel block according to the directions on pg. 16.

2. Cut a 9½" x 12½" rectangle of background fabric and sew it to the right of the Bird Circling block. This is the top row of blocks. Cut a 3½" x 8" rectangle of background fabric and sew it between the two Little Bird blocks. Sew a 2" x 21½" strip of railing fabric to the bottom of this middle row of blocks. Sew the top and middle rows together.

3. Cut:

1.	2 railing fabric	2"	strip
2.	2 floral or grass fabric	3½"	strip

4. Sew the two strips together lengthwise and cut three 12½" sections and two 3½" sections. Trim one 12½" section lengthwise by cutting off 1½" of the floral fabric. Sew the two short sections together as shown and add to the top of the squirrel block. Add the trimmed 12½" section on the right side and the other two on the left side. Add a 3½" x 21½" strip of railing across the bottom. Then sew this railing section of the quilt to the bird section.

5. Add an inner 3½" window frame border. The right side is the background value, the bottom the medium value, and the top and left the darkest value. The lower right corner can be mitered (see below) but the other three corners are straight-across seams. Complete the wall hanging with a final 2" border.

HOW TO SEW A MITERED CORNER

Cut borders somewhat longer than the length of the side of the quilt top plus the width of two borders. How much longer is determined by how wide the borders are, since the seam has to **angle** across this width, rather than go straight across. I prefer to have plenty.

1. For *My Window*, add 12" to the length of the side of these two borders (30½" becomes 42½" and 45½" becomes 57½").

2. Sew both borders on from the outside edge to the seam allowance where the two meet. Backstitch. Press.

3. On the ironing board or another flat surface, with the quilt top right side up, arrange the excess top border straight down and flat. Then fold the left side border under itself with the long tail lined up with the tail of the right side border. Tug into position until the fold forms a neat 45° angle and the edges are neatly lined up. Press firmly with an iron to set the fold. (Will also leave a line in the fabric below.) Tuck in a couple of pins through both fabrics across the fold.

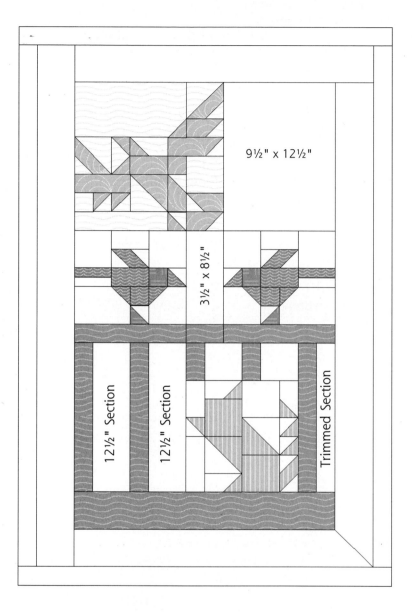

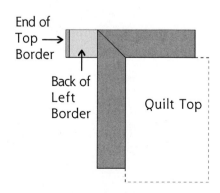

End of Top → Border

Back of Left Border

Quilt Top

4. Then fold over the left side border and part of the quilt top to see the back of the fold and the two strips of fabric over each other. Pin through the strips close to the fold, being careful not to disturb the alignment. Sew along the fold line (taking out the pins as you stitch), from the outside edge to the seam allowance. Backstitch. Check the appearance of the corner from the front. If satisfactory, trim excess fabric to a ¼" seam and press again.

OUT TO PASTURE

All fabric 42" wide prewashed.

Fabric requirements:

¼ yd. cow fabric (¼ yd. each cow if using different fabrics)

2 yds. sky fabric (2 pieces 1 yd. each)

¾ yd. grass fabric for setting strips

2½ yd. border fabric

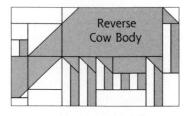

2" finished square
Quilt with borders: 70½" x 76½"

Directions:

1. Cut for **each** Cow block:

1.	1 cow	6½" x 12½"	rectangle
2.	1 background and 1 cow	4⅞"	square
3.	2 background	2½" x 6½"	rectangle
4.	1 cow	2½" x 5½"	rectangle
5.	2 background and 1 cow	2½" x 4½"	rectangle
6.	1 background and 1 cow	1½"	strip
7.	3 background and 5 cow	2½"	square
8.	1 background	1½" x 2½"	rectangle
9.	1 background	1½"	square

Reverse
Cow Body

Reverse Cow Block

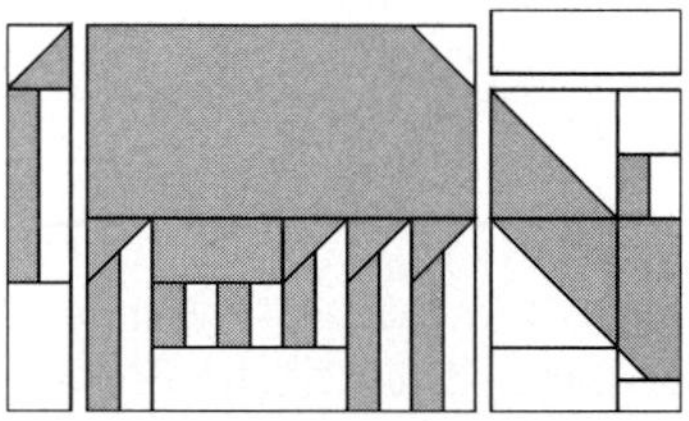

Piecing Diagram

2. Sew the background and cow 1½" strips together lengthwise. Press to the dark. Then cut the following sections from this set of strips for each block:

1.	4	6½" section
2.	1	4½" section
3.	3	2½" section

3. (A) Place a cow 2½" square on one end of a 6½" strip section as shown and sew a diagonal seam according to the diagram. Outside the stitching, trim fabric to a ¼" seam. Press to the dark. Make three of these for each Cow or **three reverse for each reverse block.** (B) Place a cow 2½" square on one end of a 4½" strip section as shown and sew a diagonal seam according to the diagram. Trim and press to the dark. Make one for each Cow or **one reverse for each reverse block.**

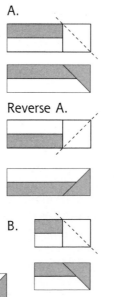

A.

Reverse A.

B.

Reverse B.

4. Place the background and cow 4⅞" squares right sides together. Draw a corner to corner diagonal line on the back of the lightest fabric. Sew a ¼" seam on both sides of the drawn line. Cut on the line to produce half-squares. Make 16 of these. Sew together to make four Cow necks and **four Reverse Cow necks.**

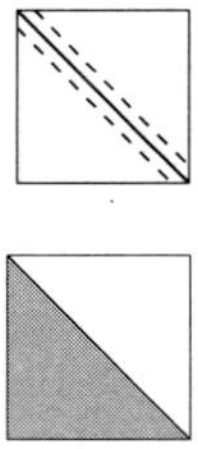

5. (C) Sew the background 1½" square on one corner of the cow 2½" x 5½" rectangle with a diagonal seam as shown. Trim and press to the dark. (D) Sew a background 2½" square on a corner of the cow 6½" x 12½" rectangle as shown. Trim and press. Make four **and four reverse** of each of these.

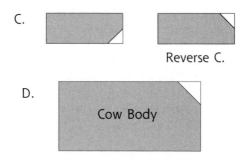

C.

Reverse C.

D.

Cow Body

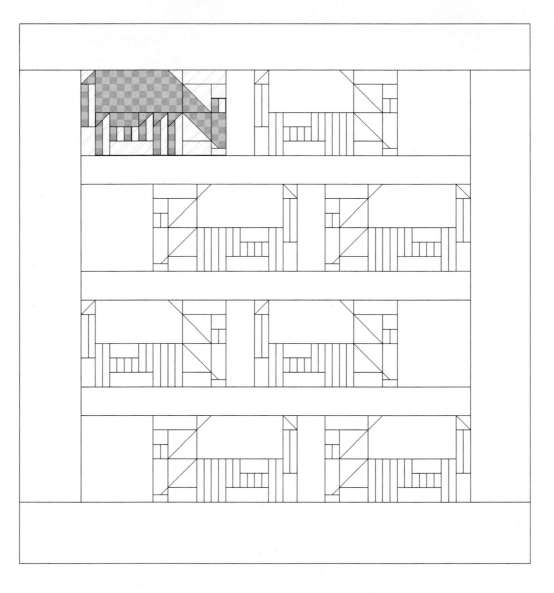

6. Place a background and cow 2½" square right sides together and sew a diagonal seam. Trim on one side of the stitching to a ¼" seam allowance. Press to the dark. Make eight of these. This is a 2½" half-square. Assemble four Cow blocks and four Reverse Cow blocks according to the piecing diagram.

7. Cut:

1.	4	4½" x 12½"	setting strip (sky)
2.	4	10½" x 12½"	setting piece (sky)
3.	3	4½" x 54½"	setting strip (grass)

8. Sew the Cow blocks and the reverse Cow blocks into four rows as shown in the quilt diagram. Sew the 4½" x 12½" sky setting strip between two Cow blocks and the 10½" x 12½" setting piece on the front of each row. Sew the rows together with three 4½" grass setting strips between them. Add a final 6¾" outer border to complete the quilt.

KANGAROO QUILT

All fabric 42" wide prewashed.
Fabric requirements:
1 yd. background fabric
¾ yd. dark kangaroo fabric
¼ yd. fabric for setting strips
½ yd. inner border fabric
½ yd. dark sawtooth fabric
½ yd. background sawtooth fabric
⅔ yd. outer border fabric

2" finished square
Quilt with borders: 52½" x 60½"

Directions:

1. Cut for four Kangaroo blocks:

1.	5 background and 5 kangaroo	1½"	strip
2.	4 background	4½" x 10½"	rectangle
3.	4 background	6½" x 8½"	rectangle
4.	2 background and 2 kangaroo	4⅞"	square
5.	8 kangaroo	4½"	square
6.	4 background	2½" x 14½"	rectangle
7.	12 background and 8 kangaroo	2½" x 4½"	rectangle
8.	16 background and 24 kangaroo	2½"	square

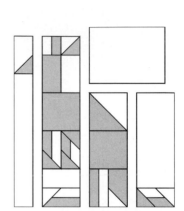

Piecing Diagram

2. Sew the 1½" background and kangaroo strips together lengthwise. Press to the dark. Cut twenty 4½" sections from this strip set (kangaroo arms, leg, and tail). Then cut four 2½" sections (kangaroo ear).

3. (A) Place a kangaroo 2½" square on one end of a 4½" strip section and sew a diagonal seam as shown. Outside the stitching, trim fabric to a ¼" seam. Press to the dark. Make eight of these. (B) Take one and place a 2½" kangaroo square on the other end. Sew the same diagonal, trim and press. Make four of these. (C) Place a background 2½" square on one end of a 4½" strip section and sew a diagonal seam as shown. Trim and press. Make four of these.

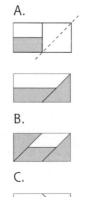

A.

B.

C.

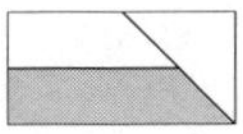

4. (D) Place a kangaroo 2½" square on one end of a 4½" strip section and sew a diagonal seam as shown. Trim and press. Place a 2½" background square on the other end. Sew the same diagonal, trim and press. Make eight of these. (E) Place a kangaroo 2½" square on a background 2½" x 4½" rectangle. Place a background square on a kangaroo rectangle. Sew each diagonally to produce the units as shown. Make four of each.

5. Place the background and kangaroo 4⅞" squares right sides together. Draw a corner to corner diagonal line on the back of the lightest fabric. Sew a ¼" seam on both sides of the drawn line. Cut on the line to produce four large half-squares.

D.

E.

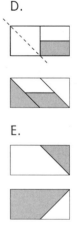

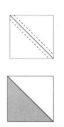

KANGAROO QUILT

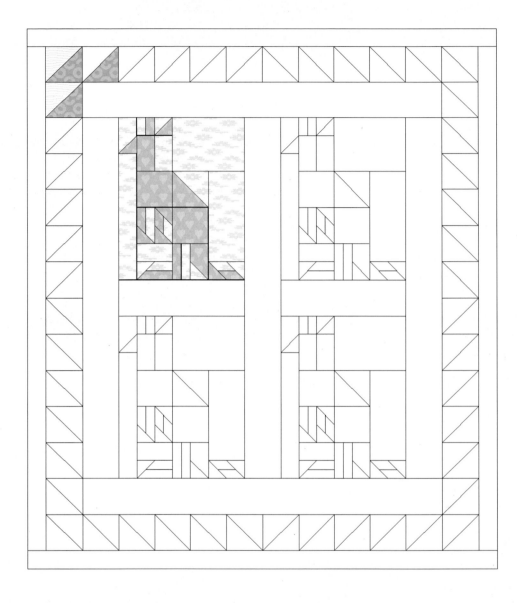

6. Place background and kangaroo 2½" squares right sides together and sew a diagonal seam. Trim one side to a ¼" seam and press to the dark. This is a 2½" half-square. Make four of these. Assemble four Kangaroo blocks according to the piecing diagram.

7. Cut two 4½" x 14" rectangles of setting strip fabric. Sew the four blocks into two rows with a setting strip between the two blocks. Sew the rows together with a 4½" setting strip between them. Sew on a 4½" inner border.

8. Cut: 24 background and 24 dark 4⅞" squares. Place one of each right sides together. Draw a corner to corner diagonal line on the back of the lightest fabric. Sew a ¼" seam on both sides of the drawn line. Cut on the line to produce half-squares. Make 48 of these. Sew 12 half-squares together for one border, six pointing left and six pointing right (they meet in the middle to produce a large triangle). Make four of these sawtooth borders. First sew on the left and right borders, then sew on the top and bottom borders. Add a final 2½" border.

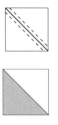

FARMYARD

┌─────────────────────────────────┐
│   1½" finished square   │
│   Quilt with borders: 55½" x 60"│
└─────────────────────────────────┘

Directions:
1. Piece 9 animal blocks as indicated below:
Cow pg. 34
Reverse Cow pg. 34
Goose pg. 5
Hen pg. 14
Reverse Pig pg. 10
Reverse Rooster pg. 15
Piglet pg. 11
Horse pg. 54
and Dog pg. 28 *(Omit the 2" x 12½" strip from the left side of the Dog block.)*

2. Cut and sew the setting strips to blocks as below:

1.	3½" x 15½"	Bottom of Cow block
2.	3½" x 15½"	Top of reverse Cow block
3.	3½" x 11"	Bottom of reverse Rooster block
4.	3½" x 11"	Bottom of Piglet block
5.	3½" x 9½"	Bottom of Goose block
6.	5" x 11"	Bottom of reverse Pig block

3. Sew the reverse Rooster block, Piglet block, and Hen block into a vertical strip as shown. Cut and sew setting strips on the right side of blocks as below:

1.	3½" x 12½"	Cow block
2.	3½" x 12½"	reverse Cow block
3.	3½" x 12½"	Goose block
4.	2" x 12½"	Dog block
5.	4¼" x 12½"	reverse Pig block
6.	4¼" x 12½"	Horse block

All fabric 42" wide prewashed.
Fabric requirements:
(Note: If each animal is a different color, as a rule of thumb allow ¼ yd. for each animal and for its background. You may use fat quarters, ⅛ yd. pieces, all kinds of scraps. This amount includes extra for shrinkage, off-grain fabrics, etc. Use leftovers to build your fabric library.)
½ yd. setting strip fabric
1 yd. inner border fabric
1⅓ yd. outer border fabric

4. Sew three horizontal rows of blocks (two blocks each) as shown in the quilt diagram.

1.	Cow	Goose
2	Reverse Pig	Horse
3.	Dog	Reverse Cow

Sew the three rows together and add the vertical row on the right side. Add a 4" inner border and a 6½" outer border to complete the quilt top.

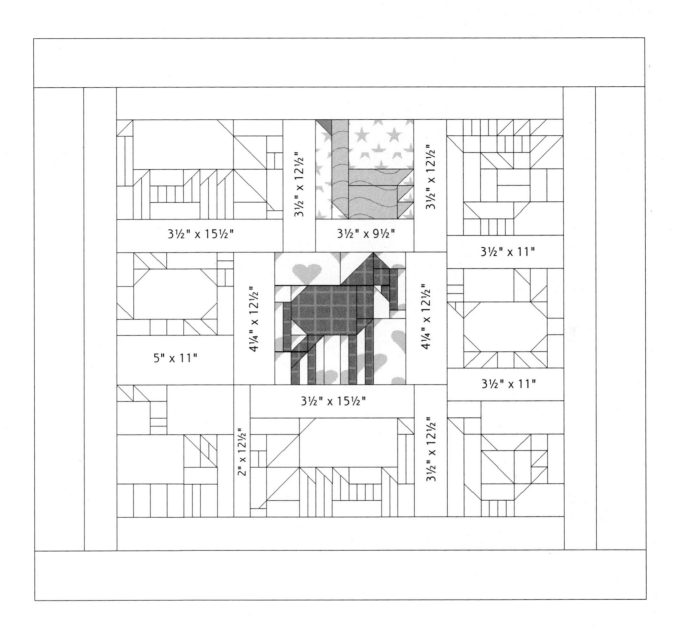

READY TO RIDE

All fabric 42" wide prewashed.
Fabric requirements:
1½ yd. horse fabric
2 yd. background fabric
2 yd. alternate squares
1¾ yd. border fabric

1½" finished square
Quilt with borders: 74½" x 86½"

Directions: 1. Piece 15 Horse blocks according to the directions on pg. 54. OR: Cut for 15 Horse blocks:

1.	15 horse	5" x 6½"	rectangle
2.	8 background and 8 horse	3⅞"	square
3.	30 background	3½" x 6½"	rectangle
4.	15 background	2" x 5"	rectangle
5.	45 background and 15 horse	2" x 3½"	rectangle
6.	12 background and 12 horse	1¼"	strip
7.	15 background	1¼" x 2"	rectangle
8.	60 background and 90 horse	2"	square

2. Piece the rest of the horse according to the directions on pg. 54. Cut 15 alternate 12½" squares. Make six rows of Horse blocks and alternate squares according to the quilt diagram. Sew the rows together and add a 7½" final border.

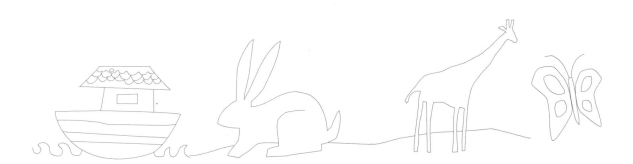

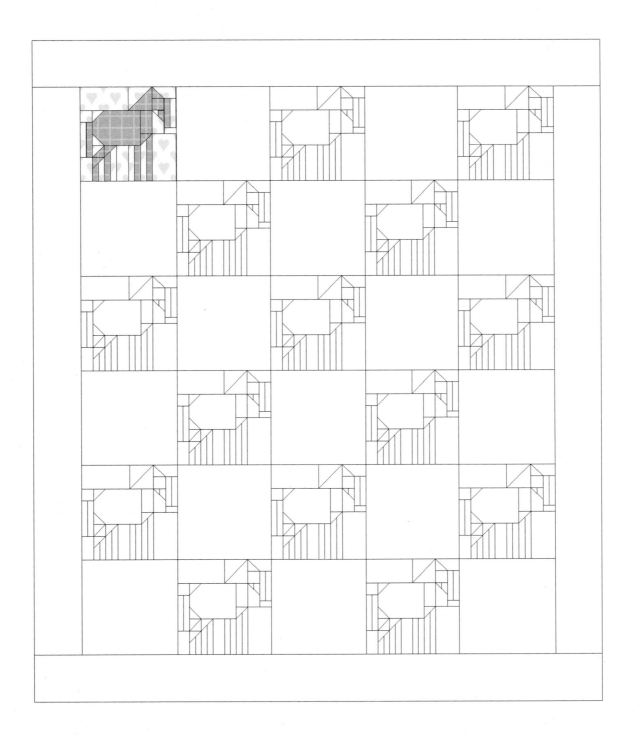

PIG PEN

All fabric 42" wide prewashed.

Fabric requirements:
½ yd. pig fabric
½ yd. background fabric
¼ yd. setting fabric
¼ yd. inner border
½ yd. red
½ yd. black
⅔ yd. white
½ yd. final border

1½" finished square
Quilt with borders: 42½" x 42½"

Directions:
1. Piece three Pig blocks according to the directions on pg. 10. OR: Cut:

1.	3 pig	5" x 8"	rectangle
2.	6 background	2" x 5"	rectangle
3.	9 background and 6 pig	2" x 3½"	rectangle
4.	1 background and 1 pig	2" x 7"	strip
5.	1 background and 1 pig	1¼" x 20"	strip
6.	18 background and 6 pig	2"	square

2. Sew the 2" x 7" background and pig strips together lengthwise. Press to the dark, then cut three 2" sections from this set of strips for the front leg. Sew the 1¼" x 20" background and dark strips together lengthwise. Press to the dark. Then cut six 2" sections for the pig's tail. (There will be some left for the piglet tail.) Continue making the Pig blocks according to the directions on pg. 10. (You will have already completed direction #3.)

3. Make one Piglet block according to the directions on pg. 11. (You will have a start on direction #3.)

4. Cut:

1.	1 setting fabric	3½" x 8"
2.	1 setting fabric	3½" x 9½"
3.	1 setting fabric	3½" x 24½"
4.	1 background	2" x 11"
5.	1 spacing strip	2" x 27½"
6.	1 spacing strip	3½" x 27½"

5. Sew the background strip on the top of one Pig block. Sew this block to the Piglet block with a 3½" x 9½" setting strip between. Sew the other two blocks together with a 3½" x 8" setting strip between. Sew the two rows together with the long setting strip between. Surround the quilt top with a 2" inner border. Then add the 2" spacing strip at the top and the 3½" spacing strip at the bottom of the quilt top.

6. Cut:

1.	5 dark	2"	strip
2.	4 light	2"	strip

7. Sew two dark strips and a light strip together lengthwise as shown at right. Press to the dark. Make two of these. Cut 2" sections (28) from this set of strips. Sew two light strips and a dark together as shown. Press to the dark. Cut 2" sections (14) from this set of strips. Sew the sections together to make 28 Nine-patch blocks. (These could be a mix of colors.) Sew six Nine-patches together for the left and right pieced borders. Sew eight Nine-patches together for the top and bottom pieced borders. Add a final 3½" plain border to complete the quilt top.

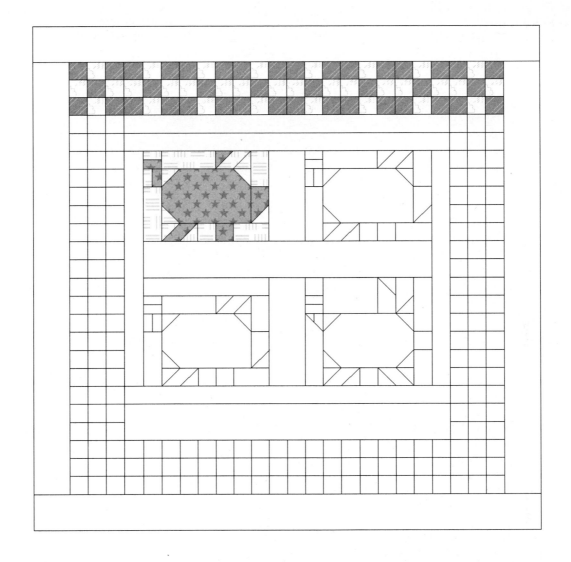

Two Sets
of Strips

Nine-Patch
Blocks

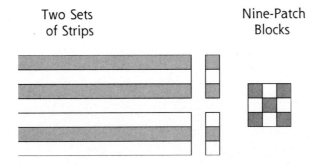

Mustangs

All fabric 42" prewashed.
Fabric requirements:
1½ yd. horse fabric (if using a
mix, ¼ yd. each horse)
1 yd. light background fabric
1½ yd. sky fabric
⅔ yd. green grass fabric
¾ yd. brown grass fabric
1¼ yd. border fabric

1½" finished square
Quilt with borders: 61" x 74"

Directions:

1. Make two Horse blocks and two Horse blocks
reversed according to the directions on pg. 54. Make
two Zebra/Horse blocks and two Zebra/Horse blocks
reversed according to the directions on pg. 27.

2. Cut:

1.	4 sky fabric	2" x 12½"	spacer strip between blocks
2.	4 sky fabric	6½" x 12½"	top section of alternate square
3.	4 sky fabric	9½" x 12½"	top section of alternate square
4.	2 green grass, 2 yellow grass	6½" x 12½"	bottom section of alternate square
5.	2 green grass, 2 yellow grass	3½" x 12½"	bottom section of alternate square
6.	1 green grass, 2 yellow grass	5" x 50"	setting strip

3. Sew the finished blocks into two sets each of blocks
and reversed blocks as shown in the quilt diagram,
putting a 2" x 12½" background vertical spacer strip
between the blocks. Then sew the alternate squares
(the author pieced them, but you could substitute
12½" x 12½" squares of fabric) and the sets of blocks
into four horizontal rows. Sew the rows and the
setting strips together with the horses facing right
and then left alternately as shown in the quilt diagram. Add a final 6½" border.

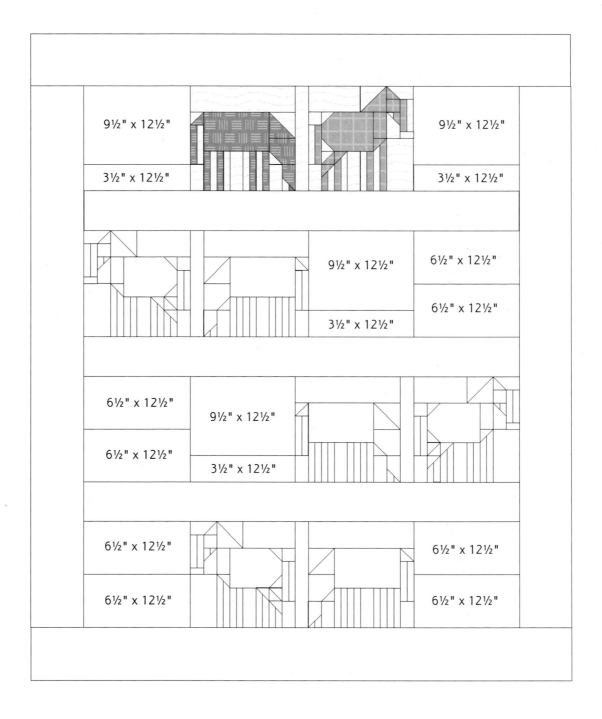

9½" x 12½"

3½" x 12½"

9½" x 12½"

3½" x 12½"

9½" x 12½"

6½" x 12½"

6½" x 12½"

3½" x 12½"

6½" x 12½"

6½" x 12½"

9½" x 12½"

3½" x 12½"

6½" x 12½"

6½" x 12½"

6½" x 12½"

6½" x 12½"

DEER CROSSING

All fabric 42" wide prewashed.
Fabric requirements:
¾ yd. deer fabric (¼ yd. each animal)
1 yd. tree fabric
⅛ yd. trunk fabric
2½ yd. background fabric
2½ yd. alternate block fabric
1¼ yd. border fabric

1½" finished square
Quilt with borders: 72½" x 83"

Directions:
1. Piece four Deer blocks according to the directions on pg. 20. Then cut:

1.	2 trunk	1¼"	strip
2.	4 background	2⅜"	strip

2. Sew one trunk and two background strips into a set of strips as shown. Make another set. Cut 34 sections 2" wide from these sets of strips. Then continue to piece 34 Christmas Tree blocks according to the directions on pg. 5.

3. Cut:

1.	34 background	5"	square
2.	17 background	2" x 11"	rectangle

Combine two 5" background squares and one 2" x 11" rectangle with two Tree blocks as shown. (This makes 11" squares with two trees in each square.) Make ten squares with the tree up on the right and seven squares with the tree up on the left.

4. Cut 21 alternate 11" squares. Sew the deer and tree squares and the alternate squares together according to the quilt diagram. Add a 5" final border.

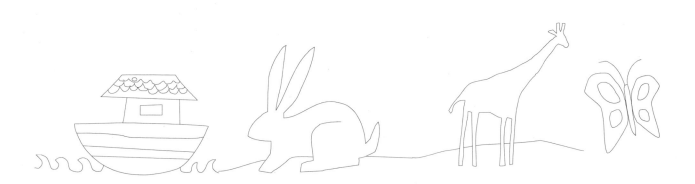

DEER CROSSING

GRIZZLY BEARS

All fabric 42" wide prewashed.
Fabric requirements:
1½ yd. bear fabric
1¼ yd. bear background fabric
1 yd. tree fabric
¾ yd. tree background fabric
⅛ yd. trunk fabric
1½ yd. horizontal setting strip fabric
1 yd. vertical setting strip fabric
1 yd. inner border fabric
1½ yd. outer border fabric

1½" finished square
Quilt with borders: 91½" x 100½"

Directions:

1. Piece six Grizzly blocks and six reverse Grizzly blocks according to the directions on pg. 61. Piece 52 Christmas Tree blocks according to the directions on pg. 5. (You can speed up the piecing of the trunk section. Cut two 2⅜" strips of your background fabric and a 1¼" strip of the trunk fabric. Sew lengthwise into a set of strips. Then cut 2" sections from this set of strips.)

2. Cut 16 vertical setting strips 3½" x 12½". Sew two Christmas Tree blocks together to make a vertical row. Sew a vertical setting strip on each side of the tree row. Make eight of these tree sections. Sew two tree sections and three bear blocks into a bear horizontal row as shown in the quilt diagram. Make two rows and two reverse rows.

3. Cut:

1.	33 tree background	2" x 6½"	rectangle
2.	6 tree background	2¾" x 6½"	rectangle

Using 12 trees, 11 background rectangles 2" x 6½", and 2 background rectangles 2¾" x 6½", assemble a tree horizontal row as shown in the quilt diagram. Make three of these.

4. Sew the bear rows and the tree rows together alternately according to the quilt diagram, placing 3½" horizontal setting strips between the pieced rows. (Pieced rows and setting strips should be about 75½" long.) Add a 3½" inner border and a final 5" border to complete the quilt.

GRIZZLY BEARS

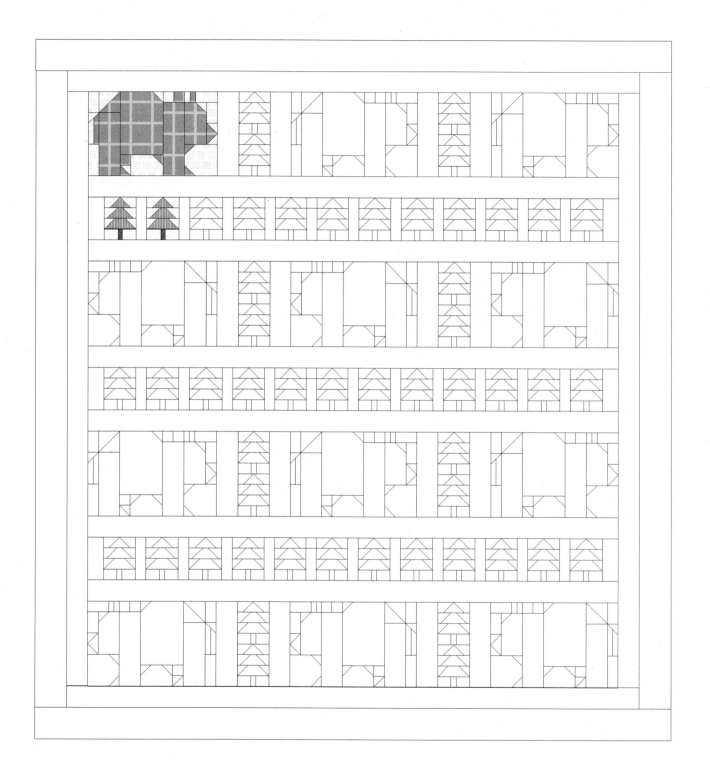

NOAH'S ARK CHILD'S QUILT

All fabric 42" wide prewashed.
Fabric requirements:
¼ yd. each animal fabric
¼ yd. each animal background fabric
¾ yd. each inner and outer setting strips
¼ yd. fabric for corner squares
1¼ yd. outer border fabric

1½" finished square
Quilt with borders: 54½" x 67½"

Directions:
1. Piece one each of the following blocks according to the directions on the pages given:

Ark, pg. 8	Giraffe, pg. 26
Scotty Dog, pg. 3	Duck, pg. 30
Pig, pg. 10	Big Squirrel, pg. 17
Deer, pg. 20	Bunny, pg. 32
Butterfly, pg. 9	Fawn, pg. 19
Hippo Yawning, pg. 7	Elephant, pg. 23

3. Cut:

1.	31	3½" x 11"	setting strips
2.	14	3½" x 11"	outer setting strips
3.	20	3½" x 3½"	corner squares*

2. Sew spacer strips on to blocks:

1.	Hippo	3½" x 11"	on bottom
2.	Fawn	2" x 11"	on right
3.	Elephant	2" x 11"	on top
4.	Scotty	2" x 9½"	on left
5.	Scotty	2" x 11"	on top
6.	Pig	3½" x 11"	on bottom

4. Assemble three blocks and four 3½" x 11" setting strips into a horizontal row as shown in the quilt diagram. Make four of these. Assemble three 3½" x 11" setting strips and four corner squares into a horizontal setting row as shown. Make five of these. Sew the horizontal rows together to make the quilt top. Add a final 5" outer border to complete the quilt. (*Or you can piece square-on-square units to use as corner squares. Cut one 3¼" square for the center and two 2⅞" squares for the corners. Cut the 2⅞" squares in half diagonally and sew the resulting triangles on all four sides of the center square.)

NOAH'S ARK CHILD'S QUILT

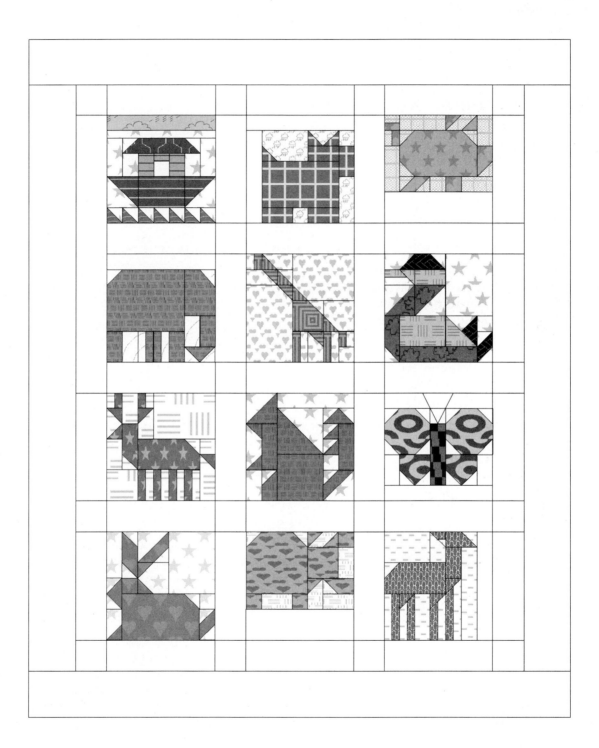

NOAH'S ARK

All fabric 42" wide prewashed.

Fabric requirements:

If each animal is a different color, as a rule of thumb allow ¼ yd. for each animal and ¼ yd. for its background fabric. You may use fat quarters, ⅛ yd. pieces, all kinds of scraps. This amount includes extra for shrinkage, off-grain fabrics, etc. Use leftovers to build your fabric library. In addition, you will need:

1 yd. Ark fabric
¾ yd. Ark sky fabric
a yd. Ark cloud fabric
⅓ yd. water fabric (2 colors)
3¼ yds. setting strip fabric
1½ yds. border fabric

1½" finished square Quilt with borders: 82¼" x 94¼"

Directions:

1. Piece 12 Ark blocks according to the directions on pg. 8. Piece one of each of the following blocks according to the directions on the pages given: *(Note: leave off the bottom strip of the Butterfly block. Also the top strip of the Bird on the Ground block should be cut at 3½" x 12½", not 5" x 12½").*

Rooster pg. 15	Monkey pg. 56
Hippo Yawning pg. 6	Zebra/Horse pg. 27
Piglet pg. 11	Bird on the Ground pg. 44
Cat pg. 12	Bunny pg. 32
Duck pg. 30	Giraffe pg. 26
Kangaroo pg. 40	Butterfly pg. 9
Rhinoceros pg. 6	Ostrich pg. 25
Goat pg. 38	Scotty Dog pg. 3
Dog pg. 28	Little Bird pg. 24

2. Add setting fabric to blocks as shown in diagram:

1.	2" x 9½"	right side	Scotty Dog
2.	2" x 9½"	left side	Little Bird
3.	2" x 15½"	left side	Ostrich
4.	water squares	bottom	Duck

3. Cut:

1.	20	3½" x 11"	setting strip
2.	5	3½" x 12½"	setting strip

4. Sew the center vertical row from six blocks as shown, alternating with the five 3½" x 12½" setting strips. Sew two vertical rows of Ark blocks, alternating with the 3½" x 11" setting strips. Sew two vertical rows of the remaining animals as shown, alternating with 3½" x 11" setting strips. (The animals can be moved to different positions in their vertical row if necessary, but they cannot be moved to another row entirely.) Sew all the rows together with 3½" setting strips between. Add an inner 3½" border of setting strip fabric, and a ¾" middle border. Complete the quilt top with a final 5½" outer border.

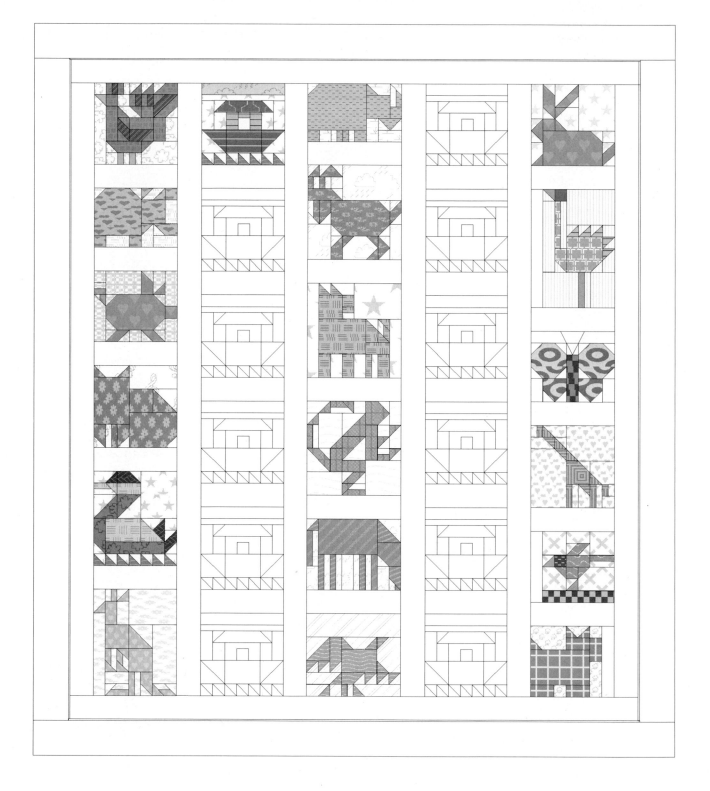

AFRICA

All fabric 42" wide prewashed.

Fabric requirements:
¾ yd. elephant fabric
¾ yd. elephant sky fabric
½ yd. giraffe fabric
1 yd. giraffe sky fabric
½ yd. zebra fabric
½ yd. zebra sky fabric
½ yd. rhino fabric
⅓ yd. rhino sky fabric
1 yd. monkey fabric
1 yd. monkey sky fabric
½ yd. hippo fabric
¼ yd. hippo sky fabric
½ yd. snake dark fabric
½ yd. snake medium fabric
1 yd. snake sky fabric
2¼ yds. setting strip fabric
1¾ yds. border fabric

Directions:

1. Make two Snake blocks according to the directions on pg. 42. Then following the directions on the pages given, make five of each of the following blocks: *(Note: you may wish to make all the strip sets from selvage to selvage cuts.)*

Bull Elephant pg. 22
Giraffe pg. 26
Zebra pg. 27
Rhinoceros pg. 6
Monkey pg. 56
Hippo Yawning Reversed pg. 7

3. Cut for setting strips between each animal:

1.	elephant	4	2" x 12½"	setting strip
2.	giraffe	4	3½" x 11"	setting strip
3.	giraffe	1	2" x 11"	setting strip
4.	zebra	4	2" x 9½"	setting strip
5.	rhinoceros	4	2" x 8"	setting strip
6.	snake	1	6½"	square
7.	monkey	4	2" x 12½"	setting strip
8.	hippo	4	3½" x 8"	setting strip
9.	hippo	1	2" x 8"	setting strip

1½" finished square
Quilt with borders: 78½" x 96½"

4. Sew the blocks and setting strips together to make horizontal rows as shown in the quilt diagram. Add a 2" x 11" setting strip on the left end of the Giraffe row and a 2" x 8" setting strip on the left end of the Hippo row. Then cut 66½" long setting strips (you may wish to measure the rows and use the average measurement) between the rows of animals. The width of these strips varies. Cut as follows:

1.	between elephant and giraffe	3½"
2.	between giraffe and zebra	2"
3.	between zebra and rhino	5"
4.	between rhino and snake	3½"
5.	between snake and monkey	5"
6.	between monkey and hippo	3½"

5. Sew all the rows and setting strips together according to the quilt diagram. Add a final 6½" border.

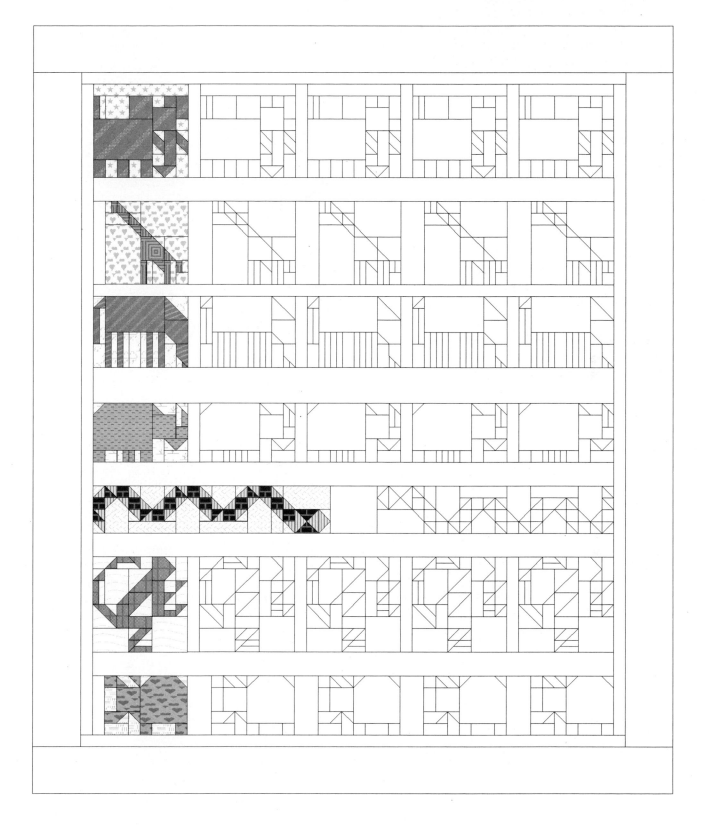

SMALL AFRICA

1½" finished square
Quilt with borders: 51½" x 51½"

All fabric 42" wide prewashed.
Fabric requirements:
¼ yd. each animal fabric
¼ yd. each animal background fabric
½ yd. fabric for setting strips
½ yd. inner border fabric
⅔ yd. outer border fabric

Directions:
1. Piece one each of the following blocks according to the directions on the pages given:
Hippo Yawning, pg. 7
Elephant, pg. 23
Giraffe, pg. 26
Rhino, pg. 6
Monkey, pg. 56
Zebra, pg. 27
Snake, pg. 42

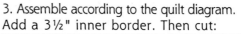

2. Add spacer strips to blocks according to chart:

1.	3½" x 11"	bottom of Giraffe
2.	3½" x 9½"	left of Hippo
3.	3½" x 12½"	bottom of Rhino
4.	3½" x 6½"	bottom of Snake
5.	2" x 6½"	top of Snake
6.	3½" x 23"*	left of Rhino and Monkey
7.	3½" x 26 "*	bottom of Elephant and Monkey
8.	3½" x 35"*	on right of Snake

*(Measure the pieced sections before cutting these long strips to match them.)

3. Assemble according to the quilt diagram. Add a 3½" inner border. Then cut:

1.	4	1¼" x 48"	inner border strip
2.	4	5" x 48"	outer border strip

4. Sew the inner border strips to the outer strips lengthwise to make four border units. Sew the first border unit onto any side of the quilt top from left to right, leaving the last inch unsewn. Sew the next border unit on in the same way, to the right of the already sewn border. Then go back and complete the first border seam, trimming the fabric. Continue sewing borders on clockwise to complete the quilt.

ANIMAL SAMPLER

All fabric 42" wide prewashed.

Fabric requirements:
(Note: As a rule of thumb allow ¼ yd. for each animal and for its background. You may use fat quarters, ⅛ yd. pieces, all kinds of scraps. This amount includes extra for shrinkage, off-grain fabrics, etc. Use leftovers to build your fabric library.)
2 yd. fabric for setting strips
1 yd. inner border fabric
1⅓ yd. outer border fabric

> 1½" finished square
> Quilt with borders: 75½" x 86"

Directions:
1. Make one of each block:

Fox pg. 29	Big Squirrel pg. 17
Horse pg. 54	Bunny pg. 32
Moose pg. 21	Hippo pg. 6
Reindeer pg. 18	Cat pg. 12
Bear pg. 58	Camel pg. 50
Kangaroo pg. 40	Flamingo pg. 36
Panda pg. 7	

2. Piece the blocks below with additions or changes as shown: *(You may wish to wait and make the additions after all blocks are pieced, then choose whether to use setting strip or other fabric instead of background fabric.)*

Deer	pg. 19	2" x 11"	rectangle of background fabric	right side
Rhinoceros	pg. 7	2" x 8"	rectangle of fabric for setting strips	right side
Giraffe	pg. 25	2" x 11"	rectangle of background fabric	right side
Owl	pg. 30	3½" x 15½"	rectangle of background fabric	right side
Zebra	pg. 26	2" x 9½"	rectangle of background fabric	left side
	and	2" x 14"	rectangle of background fabric	top
Elephant	pg. 23	* do not sew the bottom strip on the Elephant block		

3. After all the blocks are pieced, begin to assemble the quilt, adding setting strips to blocks as indicated on the quilt diagram, and in the directions below. Substitute a strip of background fabric as desired. If the fabric has a directional design, some pieces are cut vertically (length of fabric) and some are cut horizontally (width of fabric).

ANIMAL SAMPLER

4. Assemble the Animal Sampler quilt top in rows starting from the left.

Row A. Sew a 3½" x 12½" setting strip onto the bottom of the Horse block. Sew 5" x 12½" setting strips onto the bottom of the Moose and Deer blocks. Sew them into a vertical row as shown. Add a 2" setting strip on the left side of this row of blocks. Then sew the Rhinoceros block on the bottom.

Row B. Sew 3½" x 12½" setting strips onto the bottom of the Giraffe and Owl blocks. Sew the blocks together vertically as shown and add a 5" x 32" setting strip on the left side. Add a 3½" x 20" setting strip to the left side of the Bear block, and then a 3½" x 17" setting strip on the bottom of the block, and sew it onto the top of this row. Sew rows A and B together.

5. Sew a 3½" x 11" setting strip on the right side of the Fox block, and a 3½" x 18½" setting strip on the top of the block. Sew a 3½" x 14" setting strip on the right side of the Reindeer block. Sew the blocks together into a horizontal row as shown. Add a 3½" x 30½" strip onto the bottom of these two blocks. Sew this section onto the top of rows A and B.

Row C. Sew a 3½" x 14" setting strip on the right side of the Kangaroo. Sew a 3½" x 15½" setting strip on the left side of the Panda. Sew a 3½" x 11" setting strip on the left side of the Squirrel and Bunny blocks. Sew a 3½" x 9½" setting strip on the left side of the Elephant. Then sew a 3½" x 14" setting strip on the bottom of all of these except the Bunny block. Sew all five blocks together in a vertical row as shown.

Row D. Sew a 3½" x 11" setting strip on the bottom of the Hippo and the right of the Zebra. Sew a 5" x 11" setting strip on the bottom of the Cat. Sew a 3½" x 14" setting strip on the bottom of the Camel block. Sew the Hippo and Cat blocks together vertically as shown and add a 3½" x 26" setting strip on the right side. Sew the Camel block on the bottom of this section and add a 3½" x 41" setting strip on the left side of these three blocks. Sew a 5" x 15½" setting strip on the left, and a 2" x 15½" setting strip on the right of the Flamingo block and sew it on the bottom of the vertical row. Add a 5" x 17" setting strip to the bottom of the Zebra block and sew it on the top of the row. Sew rows C and D together.

6. Sew the two halves of the quilt together and add a 3½" inner border and a 5" outer border to complete the quilt.

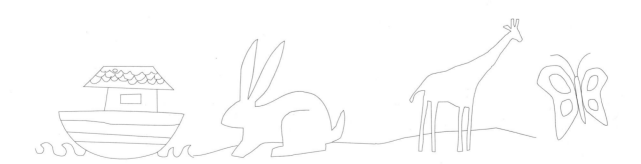

138

ANIMAL SAMPLER

CUTTING AND PIECING

General Directions
Tools

You may already have most of the tools needed to piece the quilts in this book. But they will be listed and discussed one by one below so that everything necessary is ready when you begin to make your blocks.

The **rotary cutter** is what makes these patterns quick. Choose the brand and size that is comfortable for you to use and learn how to assemble and clean it. The author prefers a middle-sized Olfa® cutter. After using your rotary cutter carefully for a while, you will no longer dull the blade with little nicks from running over pins, etc.

Rotary Cutter

You will need a **cutting mat** that will keep the rotary blade sharp and protect the table or counter top. Mats come in various colors, with or without rulings on both sides. Choose a color that is easy for you to look at. Rulings are great, but at first you may wish to check the measurements of cut pieces, as the rulings on mats are sometimes not accurate.

Mats come in many sizes, too. One of the larger sizes is good for protecting a table at home, but a smaller size works better for carrying to class. (Don't leave a cutting mat in a car on a warm day.) Eventually a well-used mat will need to be replaced. But first try turning it over and wearing out the back of the mat also.

Be sure to cut at a table or counter that's the right height for you!

There are many **rulers** that work with rotary cutters. Three favorites are the 6" x 12", the 6" square (#6A), and the 9½" square by Omnigrid®.

The 6" square is a nice size to work with.

After all the pieces are cut, you will need a sewing machine that takes a nice straight stitch, perhaps a press cloth, and an iron and ironing board.

Easy Cutting and Piecing
Strips, Squares, and Rectangles

Cut a strip first, then cut the strip into all the shapes you need. Begin by pressing prewashed fabric selvage to selvage. Then bring the fold to the selvages and press again. Use a 6" x 12" ruler to cut a strip the desired width. The short cut needed (12" rather than 24") helps keep the ruler and the rotary cutter under your control.

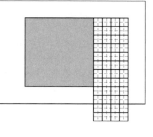

Trim edge straight, then cut the strip.

Use the top ruler edge, bottom ruler edge, or a measuring line across the ruler or on the cutting board to keep the fabric straight. Use the same ruler or perhaps a smaller square ruler to cut off the squares or rectangles needed.

TIP: If you do get a strip that's a little zig-zag, you can still cut some pieces from it (but not at the places where the strip is not straight).

Get the Most From Your Fabric

First you will usually cut a strip to match the narrowest measure of the biggest piece. Then look for other needed pieces of the same fabric that share this strip width and cut them next.

Example: The largest piece needed is a 6½" square. So you cut a 6½" strip and cut the squares. Further down the list you see a piece needed from the same fabric that measures 2½" x 6½". So you can cut 2½" wide pieces from the same width.

Then trim the strip to the next width needed, and cut as many pieces from that width as possible. Often you'll be able to get all the pieces needed out of the first strip you cut.

Tip: Also look for pieces where two will fit into the width. Say you had a strip width of 4½", and needed some pieces 2" x 6½". You could cut a piece 4½" x 6½", trim to 4", and get two of the smaller pieces from it. Generally cut all the largest pieces first, before trimming any width from the strip.

Shape Recognition

You will gradually begin to recognize the various sizes and shapes that you are cutting, and be able to pick them up as needed. But don't hesitate to check measurements with a ruler before sewing one piece on to another.

TIP: To prevent confusion when cutting pieces for a complex pattern, stack all pieces of the same size and pin them together. Write the size on a Post-It® note and stick it on top.

Square On Square™ Piecing

As always, use a ¼" seam for piecing. No small triangles are used when piecing these blocks. Instead, squares are used, and sewn diagonally onto square corners of other squares or rectangles.

For example, the cheek of the Panda (pg. 7) begins as a light strip. A square of background fabric is placed on one end of the strip, right sides together and lined up accurately. Then a seam is sewn diagonally across the square, sewing it to the larger piece. The fabrics **outside** the stitching line are trimmed to a ¼" seam and the corner pressed out.

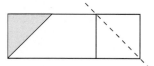

Making a Panda Cheek

Sewing and trimming both corners results in a rounded, fat cheek. These pieces are much easier to cut and to handle than little triangles and angled pieces.

The Most Important Seam

Square On Square™ piecing often requires the quilter to sew a diagonal seam across a small square. You can learn to eyeball the correct seam line, or try one of the tips below:

TIP: Draw a diagonal line on the back of the fabric square with pencil, chalk, or a wash-out marker.

TIP: Fold and crease the square from corner to corner to make a sewing line.

TIP: Use a ruler to draw a line with a permanent fine-tip marker (some colors do wear off after a while) on your sewing machine in front of the needle. The line should be perpendicular to the straight front edge of the sewing machine.

Large Half-Squares

A half-square is a square divided in half diagonally (two triangles sewn together). Usually one half is dark and the other half is light. Big triangles are relatively simple to work with. They are obtained by cutting a square the size given and then cutting the square in half diagonally using a ruler and rotary cutter.

This triangle is then sewn to a triangle of another color, to get a large half-square. This requires sewing two bias edges together. Remember to handle your fabric lightly as you are sewing the triangles together. Many sewing machines sew well straight ahead. Simply laying the two triangles right sides together and gently bringing them under the presser foot with the minimum guidance required allows the machine to do the work.

Practice makes it easier. Even if the seam gets a little stretched in sewing, pressing with a steam iron or wet press cloth generally will correct any distortion.

Small Half-Squares

In this book, small half-squares are produced by placing two small squares right sides together and sewing diagonally. The fabrics then are trimmed to a ¼" seam on one side of the stitching. The seam is pressed to the dark. If you need a lot of small half-squares made from the same fabrics, use one of the fast methods for which there are papers or templates. Example: Perfect Square™ .

Half-Square It Again

In a few of these patterns, you take the square-on-square technique one step farther. For example: the method used to make the duck's tail (pg. 30). First a half-square is produced. This is then placed on a 3½" square, right sides together, and a seam is stitched perpendicular to the seam in the half-square (Direction #1B). Care must be taken to trim the excess fabric on the **correct** side of the stitching. This is easier than cutting the half-square and square into triangles, and then seaming the triangles together.

TIP: If you need two large half-squares in the same fabrics, don't cut the light and dark squares in half. Instead, lay the light and dark squares right sides together, draw a diagonal line on the back of the light fabric square with pencil or a wash-out marker, and sew a ¼" seam each side of this line. Cut along the pencil line for two pre-sewn large half-squares.

TIP: The rule is usually to press to the dark. Occasionally bulky seams make it easier to press to the light.

Speedy Strips

Strip piecing is another way to make speed and accuracy easy. To use the Panda Bear Quilt (pg. 88) as an example, the eyes are produced by sewing together 2" x 9" white and black strips and and cutting 2" sections from this set of strips. These pieces could be all cut out separately and sewn together, but it is much easier to sew long strips together first, press them, and then cut 2" **already sewn** sections from the strip set.

TIP: After sewing the long narrow strips together, press the seams to the dark, pulling across the strips as you press to make sure no fabric measurement is lost in the seams. The tip of the iron helps. Then press along the strips, pulling the strip set out straight to correct any distortion from the previous pressing.

Chain Sewing

The author used to have a sewing machine that cut the top thread with each stitch unless there was fabric under the presser foot. So I learned to chain sew. Pieces to be sewn are fed under the needle with minimum space between, and cut apart later. This speeds up the sewing and prevents the messiness of long tails of thread draped everywhere, needing to be trimmed. Many quilters keep a piece of scrap fabric to use at the start (and end) of each chain.

Pressing Techniques

Try a wet press cloth as an alternative to the steam iron. Many experienced quilters feel that using a steam iron distorts the fabric during pressing. Use a dry iron for most of the pressing (perhaps after each seam sewn). This avoids the weight of the iron causing sore elbows and arms during extended piecing sessions.

Then when one block or unit is complete, take a piece of old sheet (my favorite, but muslin works too), dampen it in a sink, wring it out, and lay it flat over the pieced block. (The block is right side up.) Run the hot iron lightly but completely over the damp cloth to dampen the block underneath. Then lay the wet press cloth aside, and dry and flatten the block with the hot iron. You may wish to turn the block over afterwards to check that the seams are all laying correctly. Also you can tug at the block a bit as you dry it to square it up. This is like blocking a sweater. Block your block.

SPECIAL THANKS TO THESE MANUFACTURERS:

Fairfield Processing Corp.
Cotton Batting-Soft Touch® by Fairfield

Quilter's "Dream" Cotton™ Batting
Kelsul, Inc.- Cotton Batting

Fasco/Fabric Sales Co., Inc.
Fabric - Marsha McCloskey's Staples™
Fabric - Nancy Martin's Roommates™

Mission Valley Textiles
100% Cotton Yarn-dyed Woven Fabric

Hoffman California International Fabrics
Bali Collection

P&B Textiles
Fabrics-Italia Collection by Deborah Corsini

Concord House
Fabric Collections

Mallery Press
Publishers

Omnigrid, Inc.
Omnigrid® Rulers for Rotary Cutting
Omnimat®

Perfect Square© by Monica Novini
Half-square Iron-on Papers

ALSO AVAILABLE FROM CLEARVIEW TRIANGLE:

From Quick Picture Quilts - Books
MC-16	Merry Christmas	$9.95
HH-17	Happy Halloween	$9.95
NL-19	New Labels	$6.95

60° Triangle - Tools For Rotary Cutting
CT1	6" Triangle ruler	$7.00
CT2	12" Triangle ruler	$12.00
MP3	8" Triangle ruler	$10.50
GP12	Isometric Graph paper	$5.95

60° Triangle - Books
SF8	Stars & Flowers: Three-sided Patchwork	$5.00
MA14	Mock Applique'	$15.95
EE7	Easy & Elegant	$5.00
BB10	Building Block Quilts	$14.95

To Order:
Send item cost plus $2.00 s/h first item
-$1 s/h for each additional item to:
      Clearview Triangle
      8311 180th St. S. E.
      Snohomish, WA 98296-4802 USA

Toll-Free: 1- 888 - 901- 4151

Check our Website at:
http://ourworld.compuserve.com/
homepages/clearviewtriangle/index.htm